Vincent Geoghegan

Reason and Eros
The Social Theory of Herbert Marcuse

Pluto  Press

First published 1981 by Pluto Press Limited,
Unit 10 Spencer Court, 7 Chalcot Road, London NW1 8LH

Copyright © 1981 Vincent Geoghegan

ISBN 0 86104 335 9

Cover designed by Clive Challis A.Gr.R.
Typeset by Grassroots Typeset, London NW6 Tel: 328 0318
Printed in Great Britain by
The Camelot Press Limited, Southampton

Contents

Preface

I would like to thank the following for their invaluable help in reading and criticising earlier drafts of this book: Mike Ashley, Graeme Duncan and Phil Lawrence; also those who similarly read and criticised the research work of which the book is a product: David George, David Goodman, Graeme Duncan, Peter Jones, David McLellan, David Miller and, above all, Tim Gray. Any errors which remain have been perpetrated by the author alone. Thanks are due also to Richard Kuper of Pluto Press who encouraged me to write the present book and improved it greatly by his criticism; to Hugh Berrington's excellent Department of Politics at the University of Newcastle-upon-Tyne; and to the SSRC for funding the earlier research.

I would also like to acknowledge the 'management' of the University of East Anglia, who provided me with the 'leisure' to write this work ...

Finally, the work literally could not have been written without the help and encouragement of John Le Juen, to whom it is dedicated.

Introduction

Looking back on the late 1960s Marcuse often recalled the surprise he had felt at finding himself elevated at the age of seventy to international fame. His seemed the name of the moment, inextricably linked to the great upheavals which were taking place, chanted in demonstrations, daubed on walls, condemned in high places. It is worth quoting a couple of extracts which admirably convey the Marcusemania of that period:

> Through what the French, in a delightful phrase, call 'la drugstorisation de Marcuse', he has himself become something of a commodity. No article on the New Left is complete without a ritual mention of his name; no discussion of the 'counter culture' dares ignore his message of liberation.[1]

> Amost overnight the unknown dialectician became, in Fortune's phrase, the 'improbable guru of surrealist politics' and simultaneously evoked the wrath of authorities and authoritarians everywhere. Indeed, it is one of the unique achievements of Marcuse's work that it has unified California's right-wing elders, *Pravda*, liberals such as Irving Howe and Nathan Glazer, the French Communist Party, and, most recently, the Pope in a single chorus of reprobation against the supposed pied piper who has corrupted the minds, morals and manners of the young.[2]

A little over a decade later the picture is very different. Amongst the left, when he is mentioned at all, Marcuse is usually spoken of as a phase gone through, a dose of theoretical acne, the product of youthful folly, long surpassed by mature preoccupations — structuralism, for example. Though much could be written on the causes and nature of the rise and fall of the 'Marcuse phenomenon', this little work does not set out to do so; its starting point is a belief that throughout this riches to rags story the actual strengths and weaknesses of Marcuse's work have all too often been overlooked, eclipsed by the absurd positions of an apocryphal Marcuse — the Marcuse who claimed that students were the new proletariat, or who called for the end of technology or advocated sex with rocks! The aim of this work is therefore modest — to present the social theory of Herbert Marcuse clearly, accurately and sympathetically through an exposition of his theoretical output and the various influences which shaped it.

Familiarity with the work of Marcuse is indispensable to anybody who is seriously interested in a comprehensive and living marxism for his work focuses on areas which are of fundamental importance to marxists. As two otherwise far from sympathetic critics, Walton and Gamble, have said of him: 'The problems he raises ... are undoubtedly important ones for a modern marxist theory ... He has asked all the right questions.'[3] To detail here the nature of these problems and questions, and Marcuse's particular solutions and answers, would be to preempt the rest of the book; however it is worth outlining very generally at this stage the principal contribution which Marcuse made to marxism.

It is a token of the dominance of scientism within contemporary marxist theory that the central concern of Marcuse's marxism might seem naive and unsophisticated — a concern articulated in his very first published article in the form of a question: what is authentic existence, how is it possible? This question was raised by marxists as the development of nineteenth-century advanced capitalism shattered the optimism of orthodox revolutionary marxism with its centrepiece of the revolutionary proletariat. In the uncertainty created by the unproblematic becoming problematic, Marcuse was one of those who looked long and hard at the nature of, and relationship between, the means and the end of revolutionary marxism, a process which involved him throughout his life in three broad areas of enquiry: firstly, investigation into the philosophical (particularly the ontological) basis of marxism; secondly, into the nature of the revolutionary subject; and finally, into the obstacles hindering the emergence of authentic existence.

With respect to the first of these areas Marcuse sought, through the work of the early Marx and a host of pre-marxist and non-marxist artistic and intellectual traditions, to develop a conception of authentic existence. He deplored those currents in marxism which saw in communism a simple negation of individualism or which made the necessary economic and social preconditions of communism sufficient as a definition of communism, and argued that a theory of individual realisation was present in the work of the early Marx and that it served as the basis on which all of Marx's subsequent work was grounded. As part of his major contribution to the rediscovery of 'humanism' in marxist theory Marcuse integrated insights from many diverse traditions — philosophical, anthropological, psychological, artistic, historical, mythological — into a particularly challenging vision of human possibilities.

Marcuse's distinctive marxism emerged with particular clarity in his strictures on the nature of the revolutionary subject. His conception of authentic existence referred to and connected all the phases of the transition to socialism in its rejection of the notion that authentic existence will somehow spring mysteriously forth in post-revolutionary society without first manifesting itself in pre-revolutionary society. The revolutionary subject must necessarily anticipate in its praxis the essence of the life to come prior to the universalisation of that life; the mere collapse of capitalism or seizure of power by the proletariat is no guarantee of socialism, which above all requires a self-conscious revolutionary subject. Marcuse's particular achievement was to greatly broaden the definition of the self-conscious revolutionary subject to include dimensions neglected in the marxist tradition: the role of the erotic in revolutionary praxis, for example. Theodore Roszak, writing

3

in the late 1960s, pointed to the marxism that Marcuse, in sound dialectical manner, was both reacting against and seeking to incorporate into a new synthesis:

> It is a literature of seriousness and grim resolve, tightly bounded by practicality, class discipline, the statistics of injustice, and the lust for retribution. To speak of the ecstasies of life in such a somber environment is to risk folly. Here where all men trudge, none may dance. Dancing is ... for later.[4]

The comprehensiveness which characterised Marcuse's analysis of the obstacles to the emergence of authentic existence reflected his belief that social formations are total systems whose essential natures are to be grasped through their interdependent parts: the heroes and heroines of a society's fiction, the methodology of its science and philosophy, the form of its architecture, the level of its technology (to take just a few of the phenomena analysed in *One-Dimensional Man*) were all held to be vital clues in unravelling the mystery of that society. Of particular note in Marcuse's analysis of the retardation of revolutionary praxis was his attempt to get to grips with that traditional lacuna in marxist theory — the role of the human psyche. For those who are concerned with the link between what has become known as 'the personal and the political', Marcuse's analysis is indispensable, for it is imbued with the conviction that what individuals do to each other at the sexual and interpersonal level is fundamentally linked to their behaviour at all other levels, including the political.

This brief account represents only the barest bones of Marcuse's rich and multi-faceted social theory. In the following pages I hope that these bones will eventually become fleshed out and spring to life. If they do not, it is my fault, not Marcuse's.

1. Authenticity and Labour

Herbert Marcuse was born in Berlin on 19 July 1898;[1] his parents, Carl Marcuse and Gertrud Kreslawsky, were members of the Jewish middle class which produced the majority of the future Frankfurt School. The young Marcuse appears to have developed socialist beliefs by 1917, for in that year he joined the Social Democratic Party of Germany (the SPD). In those closing years of the first world war, Marcuse did military service and, as a soldier, participated in events which he later claimed to have marked the beginning of his revolutionary commitment — the revolution of 1918-19. Although a member of a soldiers' soviet in Berlin, he remained in the SPD and joined neither the more radical Independent Social Democrats (the USPD) nor Luxemburg's Spartakusbund. However the murder of Rosa Luxemburg and Karl Liebknecht in 1919 revealed to him the clear counter-revolutionary direction of the party to which he belonged, and he resigned from it. And so ended Marcuse's first and only membership of a political party.

For the next 14 years Marcuse was, in his own words, 'relatively dormant politically'.[2] His several years of study at the universities of Berlin and Freiburg covered the fields of comparative literature, philosophy and economics, and in 1923 he produced a doctoral thesis dealing with the theme of artists in novels. During the next six years he worked for a Berlin publisher. This period witnessed the publication of his own first work — a bibliography of Schiller.[3] In 1929 he returned to academic life in Freiburg, and began studying with the leading phenomenologists of the day — Husserl and Heidegger. The year before he had produced his very first article, which contains our earliest published statement of Marcuse's marxism prior to his joining the Institute of Social Research (the nascent Frankfurt School) in 1933.[4]

This first article, entitled 'Contributions to a Phenomenology of Historical Materialism', was a product of the renaissance of marxist theory, initiated by Georg Lukács and Karl Korsch against the degenerate marxism of the second international (and ultimately of the third), and it shows Marcuse's early search for an adequate marxism. The article is linked to Marcuse's later work through its attempt to enrich marxist theory from non-marxist traditions, the source of enrichment being in this instance the work of Heidegger — particularly the latter's *Being and Time*, which had been published the previous year. The details of Marcuse's account of Heidegger's supposed contributions to a richer marxism need not concern us here. What is however important is that the central and enduring concern of Marcuse's social theory emerges in what he considered to be the fundamental validity of Heidegger's work — namely the raising of the question of the possibility and nature of authentic existence:

> One can certainly raise countless objections to Heidegger's analyses and also reject his methodological approach. But this kind of criticism misses the meaning of the work, which remains 'true', even though it contains a considerable amount of error. What is important is the new philosophical direction of his interpretations. The fundamental question of all living philosophy is raised in the light of the awareness of its utmost necessity: what is authentic existence and how is it at all possible?[5]

For Marcuse, Heidegger's work pointed beyond bourgeois philosophy to marxism, which was the only means of adequately grasping both the essence of authentic existence and the process of its realisation through praxis; throughout the various changes Marcuse's work underwent over the years the question of what authentic existence is and how it can be achieved remained the primary concern of his social theory.

It appears that Marcuse's ultimate goal on his return to

Freiburg was to obtain a university teaching post, for he prepared a Habilitation thesis, the prerequisite for such a post. Ironically perhaps, it was in the years up to 1933 — the bulk of which he spent working with Heidegger — that he partially emancipated his thinking from the influence of the phenomenologist. A number of factors were responsible for this.

In the first place, Marcuse had never been an uncritical disciple of Heidegger. His marxist perspective enabled him to pinpoint the major defects in his teacher's work. Heidegger, according to Marcuse, was totally unaware of 'the material constitution of historicity'. In other words, Marcuse believed that Heidegger failed to see that modern society was divided into economically-based classes and consequently, that Heidegger was blind to the most important determining element in human society. The political consequences of this were obvious in that Heidegger was unable to see the emancipatory role of the proletariat and misguidedly believed that isolated, individualistic solutions were possible for overcoming the malaise of modern society. Heidegger, Marcuse claimed in his 1928 article, 'ends up with solitariness rather than with solidarity'.[6]

Heidegger's flirtation with national socialism was another factor in Marcuse's self-distancing from phenomenology. Initially, Marcuse felt the effect of this move on his teacher's part at the personal rather than the theoretical level, in that increasing tension between Heidegger and his left-wing Jewish student culminated in Marcuse leaving Freiburg in 1932, unable to obtain sponsorship for his Habilitation. Its ultimate effect on Marcuse at the theoretical level was twofold: firstly it showed him how phenomenology (and especially its existentialist derivatives) could develop crude apologies for fascism. This however should not be overstressed.[7] Marcuse always maintained that Heidegger's *Being and Time* contained radical insights that pointed beyond bourgeois philosophy, and he was willing to defend Heidegger against many of the criticisms of his Frankfurt School colleagues. More importantly his search for employment led him into the Institute of Social Research (the Frankfurt School) and to the hegelian marxism which was crucially to affect his thinking.

The final factor in Marcuse's partial emancipation from Heidegger was the first publication (1932) of Marx's *Economic and Philosophical Manuscripts*, which he described in a review that same year as 'a crucial event in the history of marxist studies'.[8] The manuscripts revealed to Marcuse that Marx himself had adequately provided a philosophical basis for his revolutionary theory, which Marcuse had looked to Heidegger to provide. The *Economic and Philosophical Manuscripts* clearly showed that Marx's confrontation with Hegel's philosophy had provided the requisite depth and had made Heidegger's contribution largely redundant:

> These manuscripts could put the discussion about the origins and original meaning of historical materialism, and the entire theory of 'scientific socialism', on a new footing ... we are dealing with a philosophical critique of political economy and its philosophical foundation as a theory of revolution.[9]

These then were the factors which resulted in Marcuse's gradual, though by no means total, emancipation from Heidegger's influence in the years up to 1933, when he joined the Frankfurt School. By then his search for the philosophical roots of marxism had produced a peculiar amalgam of concepts drawn from Marx, Heidegger, Hegel, and as we shall see, even earlier sources. Underlying Marx's revolutionary theory, Marcuse glimpsed a philosophical anthropology in which the concept of labour played a crucial role; and it is to this critical reconstruction that we must now turn.

In his Habilitation thesis *Hegels Ontologie und die Grundlegung einer Theorie der Geschichtlichkeit*[10] (published in 1932), Marcuse indicated that an ontological concept of labour was present in Hegel's writings. For Hegel, labour was the means whereby individuals convert the objective world into a world for themselves. Individuals work on objectivity and transform it from an alien presence into a manifestation of themselves. The *Economic and Philosophical Manuscripts* revealed to Marcuse that Marx had grasped Hegel's vital insight in this respect. Marx, in Marcuse's reading, had seen that labour is 'the real expression and realisation of the human essence'.[11] Marx had developed this further by showing that labour was not only concretised in intellectual labour but also in non-intellectual labour, and by his valuable distinction between alienated and non-alienated labour. Marcuse felt that Marx's analysis needed fleshing out, and thus he added three new elements.

The first element[12] emerged from Marx's distinction in *Capital III* between the realm of necessity and the realm of freedom, where the former denotes the immutable struggle of the human species with nature to achieve essential material production and reproduction and the latter denotes the human activity beyond the provision of such necessities. For Marcuse, labour in the realm of necessity could never be as fulfilling as in the realm of freedom for it is labour in which one is 'forced' to participate whether one wishes to or not. According to Marcuse, even in the realm of freedom some modes of labour would be 'higher' and more fulfilling than others, the intellectual mode of labour (creation in arts, sciences etc.) being the 'highest'.

The second new element he introduced was the notion of labour as 'burden'. To Marcuse, labour would always be a burden. This because the objective world can never lose completely its alien relationship to the human subject. The gap between self and non-self can never be finally bridged and therefore the latter will tend to make demands on the former. In the labouring process the subject has always to orientate itself to the object and consequently ceases to be totally self-determining. Labour can never be the realm of total freedom:

> human doing stands under an alien, imposed law: the law of the 'thing' that is to be dealt with ... In labor one is always distanced from one's self-being and directed toward something else; one is always with others and for others.[13]

This obtains even in what Marx would have described as unalienated labour, for it is rooted in 'the structure of being typical of human existence' and not simply in a particular mode of production. For Marcuse, labour could never be totally unalienated.

There was, however, according to Marcuse, an activity that is neither labour nor burdensome in nature, and this was the third new element — play. In play, one frees oneself from the alien quality of objects by totally determining them. By contrast with labour, in play one can do exactly what one likes to objects: they cease to have a say in what is done to them. Play, therefore, involves a freedom not present in labour:

> While playing, one does not conform to objects ... in this self-positing transcendence of objectivity one comes precisely to oneself, in a dimension of freedom denied in labor. In a single toss of a ball, the player achieves an infinitely greater triumph of freedom over objectification than in the most powerful accomplishment of technical labor.[14]

At this stage of his life Marcuse was not willing, as he was later, to consider play the quintessential mode of human existence. The role of play in this period was a purely subordinate one. Unlike labour, play lacks duration and permanence. It has no role in itself, being simply the cessation of, and preparation for, labour.

These then were the main elements of the philosophical anthropology underlying Marcuse's marxism when he joined the Frankfurt School in 1933. Since Marcuse's membership of this organisation was to be so important in the development of his thought, it is necessary to give a brief outline of the history of this body and the circumstances which led Marcuse to join it.[15]

What has since become known as the Frankfurt School started life in 1923 as the Institute of Social Research. Its founder, Felix Weil, wanted it to be a body of marxist scholars engaged in research in a wide range of disciplines, though he particularly stressed the need for work on the philosophical basis of historical materialism. Under Grünberg, the Institute's first director, this philosophical component was somewhat eclipsed by historical and economic studies and it was not until 1930 and the directorship of Max Horkheimer that philosophical concerns came to the fore. In 1932 an unemployed Marcuse was introduced to Horkheimer by Kurt Riezler of the University of Frankfurt at the behest of Husserl. Marcuse's published Habilitation thesis had been reviewed by Adorno, another major figure in the Institute, who had disliked the influence of Heidegger in the work but had realised that Marcuse was moving towards the hegelian marxism of Horkheimer and himself. In January 1933, Hitler came to power, thus making the Institute's position in Germany problematic in the extreme. Horkheimer therefore dropped an idea he had of offering to sponsor Marcuse's Habilitation in Frankfurt. Instead, he made him an associate member of the Institute and sent him immediately to the Geneva office as the whole Institute began a long exile, the bulk of which was spent in the USA. In 1934 Marcuse arrived in the United States, where he was to reside for the remaining 45 years of his life.

2. Critical Rationality

Between 1934, when he arrived in the USA, and 1942 when he began an eight-year stretch with the Office of Intelligence Research in the State Department, Marcuse laid the theoretical foundations of his mature social theory. He was to retain many of the positions he had developed before 1934, integrating these with the perspectives he obtained from his colleagues at the Institute of Social Research — the most influential of which, with respect to his social theory, were Horkheimer and Adorno.

The single, most important element of theoretical continuity in this period of transition was the centrality of humanism in his social theory. In the years before he joined the Institute, he had strenuously denied the validity of any attempt to divide the work of Marx into an early, philosophical period and a later, scientific (i.e. non-philosophical) one. He maintained that the humanism of the *Economic and Philosophical Manuscripts* of 1844 was not a youthful aberration but the real basis of all Marx's subsequent work. In 1933 he wrote of Marx:

> It is useless to reject his foundation of economic theory, especially as it is worked out in the *Economic and Philosophic Manuscripts* of 1844 and in *The German Ideology* as the philosophical sins of youth that were later overcome. Such a foundation is operative throughout *Capital*, and is explicitly taken up in crucial places.[1]

His belief that humanism was a desideratum of an adequate social theory was not to be shaken by his period at the Institute, for he was to argue in *Reason and Revolution*, published at the very end of his Institute days, that the 'idea of the full realization of the individual' had regrettably been lost in the marxist tradition.[2] However, the period at the Institute did deepen his perception of what actually separated the young from the mature Marx, to the extent that he explicitly warned against excessive concentration on the works of the former: 'Marx's early writings are mere preliminary stages to his mature theory, stages that should not be over-emphasized'.[3] It may nonetheless be argued that Marcuse's mature social theory owed far more to the methods and concerns of the early Marx than it did to the mature critique of political economy. With this in mind, we shall begin our analysis with Marcuse's humanism.

In 1928, Marcuse had applauded Heidegger's concern with what he characterised as 'the fundamental question of all living philosophy', namely: 'What is authentic existence, and how is it at all possible?'[4] Before 1934, he conceived of authentic existence in terms of Marx's concept of labour, and despite the doubts of his new colleagues, Horkheimer and Adorno, he retained this belief in the ontological significance of labour; in *Reason and Revolution*, for example, he organised his presentation of Marx's work around this concept.

For Marcuse, labour both expressed and realised the essence of the human species. Essence is an important and constantly recurring concept in his work and is drawn from a deeprooted tradition of thought in western philosophy, the origins of which lie with the Greeks; the importance of this concept in Marcuse's work derived from his characterisation of reality as 'negative', a conception heavily influenced by his reading of Hegel. According to Marcuse, that which exists is not what it should and could become, and consequently, reality is indicted by its potential. Using an implicitly value-laden analysis, he distinguished between true and false forms of reality, in which the former is characterised as the essence. Thus, if we return to the statement that labour realises and expresses the human essence, we find that Marcuse defined Marx's concept of the human essence as humanity's faculties, powers and needs; and

13

in a 1936 essay, he used and expanded this to define the human essence as being all the achievements of individuals in history which have contributed to human happiness, combined also with conceivable (but as yet non-existent) forms of human happiness:

> All historical struggles for a better organization of the impoverished conditions of existence, as well as all of suffering mankind's religious and ethical ideal conceptions of a more just order of things, are preserved in the dialectical concept of the essence of man ... There can also be experience of potentialities that have never been realized.[5]

The influence of the work of Wilhelm Dilthey can be detected here. Dilthey's important role in the history of hegelian marxism has not received the attention which it deserves; the two early giants of the Hegel revival, Korsch and Lukács, both acknowledged their debt to this thinker, whose book on the young Hegel *Die Jungendgeschichte Hegels* (1906) stimulated new interest in Hegel. Marcuse's pre-Institute work revealed a clear Dilthean presence, not simply through Heidegger's own appropriation of Dilthey, but directly. Thus in his 1928 article on the possibility of a phenomenology of historical materialism, Marcuse used Dilthey as a corrective to Heidegger's failure to confront the socio-economic basis of actual history, commending Dilthey's insistence on the importance to a correct historical understanding of acknowledging the brute facts of race, nation and power relations.[6] In a 1931 article 'Das Problem der geschichtlichen Wirklichkeit', Marcuse praised Dilthey for his famous distinction between *Naturwissenschaften* (natural sciences) and *Geisteswissenschaften* (cultural sciences), a distinction that served as the basis for Marcuse's own attack on Engels's dialectics of nature in that article. Dilthey's concept of life (*Leben*) with its notion of humanity as the creating and comprehending subject of history was similarly endorsed.[7] Marcuse's 1932 Habilitation thesis is steeped in the work of Dilthey, and indicates the importance of the latter's reading of Hegel to his own understanding of that thinker — and this importance continued, for Dilthey's book on Hegel is referred to favourably in *Reason and Revolution*.[8]

At the centre of Dilthey's work was the notion, which Marcuse absorbed, that humankind can only understand itself by looking at the way it has manifested itself in history. Dilthey's formulation was that:

> man does not understand his own self by means of any kind of rumination upon himself ... only through an understanding of the historical reality generated by him does he obtain a consciousness of his capacities, for good or for ill.[9]

The human species is unique in its ability to create and to understand creation. History is therefore the process of the self-creation of humanity, a process understandable to individuals because of the ultimate identity of all human beings.

As labour is alienated in capitalism, individuals are unable to express and realise this essence; this state of affairs can only be overcome by the destruction of alienated labour. Marcuse criticised the marxist tradition for failing to see that the expression and realisation of human essence is the ultimate goal, and for fetishising the means to that goal — means such as the abolition of private property, or the growth of the productive forces.

We can perhaps cast more light on Marcuse's concept of human essence by examining Marx's attitude towards it. There is clearly a strand of thought in Marx's work which involves the belief that scientific analysis of specific modes of production renders invalid, as an analytical tool, the concept of human essence, in that each mode of production produces its own individuals who differ from the individuals produced by other modes; and that it is consequently illegitimate to try and isolate as a supposedly common denominator the human essence which is present in all modes of production. Thus, whilst there are capitalists and proletarians, lords and serfs, there is no essential humanity. This strand of thought became increasingly important the further Marx moved from his youthful work, and an instance can be seen in his preface to the first German edition of *Capital I*, where he said that in this work:

> individuals are dealt with only insofar as they are the personifications of economic categories, embodiments of particular class-relations and class-interests. My standpoint, from which the evolution of the economic formation of society is viewed as a process of natural history, can less than any other make the individual responsible for relations whose creature he socially remains, however much he may subjectively raise himself above them.[10]

Marcuse's concept of the human essence is used in a normative fashion (though for reasons which I shall discuss later Marcuse was loathe to admit this), and I would argue that this is a desideratum of any radical social theory and that it can be clearly seen in Marx's work. Marx, it seems to me, did use a concept of human essence as a norm throughout his work: explicitly as 'species-essence', 'species-being', and 'universal essence' in his early works; explicitly but shorn of its Hegelian terminology in the *Grundrisse*; and, finally, implicitly in the mature economic works.[11] In many respects this trend of thought is somewhat at odds with that which I mentioned above, for Marx does seem to have used a concept of human essence which was based upon, but cannot be reduced to, empirical individuals; although he used this concept principally as an ethical device, it was never totally rejected as a transhistorical analytical concept.

Returning to our exposition of Marcuse's concept of labour, he called for the abolition of labour and cited Marx as an authority for this demand, thus apparently contradicting his belief in the ontological significance of labour. This contradiction disappears when it is seen that Marcuse's 'abolition' is really Hegel's *Aufhebung*, which means the simultaneous ending of a form and the preservation of its 'truth' at a higher level. The ontological function of labour will thus be carried over into communist society. Marx, he claimed, thought that the mode of labour in the latter society would be of such a radically different nature that he 'hesitated to use the term "labor" to designate alike the material process of capitalist and of communist society'.[12] Paradoxically, in the light of our remarks on the influence of the early Marx on Marcuse's work, he used the remarks of the mature Marx concerning the question of labour in communist society to undermine the 'utopian' perspective of the younger Marx. Thus the distinction derived from *Capital III* between the realm of necessity and the realm of freedom was used to stress the inevitability of a degree of unfulfilment in any society. It is worth quoting Marx's expression of this distinction for, in one form or another, it recurs constantly in Marcuse's work:

> the realm of freedom actually begins only where labour which is determined by necessity and mundane considerations ceases; thus in the very nature of things it lies beyond the sphere of actual material production. Thus as the savage must wrestle with Nature to satisfy his wants, to maintain and reproduce life, so must civilised man, and he must do so in all social formations and under all possible modes of production.[13]

In no way will the abolition of labour proclaimed in *The German Ideology* entail the elimination of the struggle with nature and the consequent unhappiness:

> the struggle with the 'realm of necessity' will continue with man's passage to the stage of his 'actual history', and the negativity and the contradiction will not disappear.[14]

In this period, Marcuse dropped his pre-Institute belief in a 'hierarchical order' of modes of labour. Even at that time, his defence had been somewhat shamefaced, for he had asserted that it was the Greeks 'under whose influence we remain' who had developed such a hierarchy and that he was willing to maintain it' although no longer with such a good conscience!'[15] The concept of labour as burden survives implicitly in a modified form in Marcuse's belief that even in the realm of freedom there will be an element of unhappiness persisting on account of the mode of existence of human beings: that is, they are finite creatures in a changing world: 'As long as the world is mutable there will be enough conflict, sorrow, and suffering to destroy the idyllic picture.'[16] Subject and object can never become totally united except in idealist philosophy.

At the centre of the normative element which underlies Marcuse's concept of the human essence is the concept of Reason. Reason had a two-fold meaning to Marcuse, as it is both a mental faculty and a norm. We shall examine the former meaning first.

Following Kant and Hegel, Marcuse distinguished Reason (*Vernunft*) from Understanding (*Verstand*). Understanding is incapable of grasping reality, since it is unaware of the negativity that characterises reality; and, like a snapshot of a moving subject, it freezes the dynamic process or 'negative totality' which is reality. It is also fundamentally passive in that it fails to see that essence and appearance do not immediately coincide and, consequently, it accepts the given at its own valuation. Reason, however, grasps the complex process of reality by distinguishing essence from appearance; it is aware that the given is not what it should and could be.[17] For Marcuse, Reason's ontological distinction between essence and appearance necessarily involved an ethical distinction between 'is' and 'ought'. Reason thus has a second meaning in its role as the repository of what ought to be, and it therefore serves as a critical tribunal before which the given is judged and altered: 'What exists is not immediately and already rational but must rather be brought to reason'.[18]

The centrality of the concept of critical rationality in his social theory presented Marcuse with a major theoretical headache: for how was the 'truth' of this concept guaranteed? He vehemently rejected the notion that truth was relative, for critical rationality enshrines verities which are true regardless of when, how and why they were formulated. That humanity should be happy is not a relative but a universal absolute. However, he was equally opposed to what he saw as excessive 'apriorism', namely the belief that truth is a substance which can be grasped by intuition regardless of place or time, since this violated the historical materialist premise that consciousness is a product of the interaction between individuals and the world. His concept of truth was considerably influenced by Horkheimer's reading of Hegel, for Horkheimer maintained that with the passing of God there can be no claim to absolute truth — yet this in no way implies that truth is relative. At one level truth grows historically out of the constant theoretical and practical critique of partial truths:

> by ceasing to be a closed system, the dialectic does not lose the stamp of truth. In fact, the disclosures of conditional and one-sided aspects of other thought and its own forms an important impetus to the intellectual process. Hegel and his materialist followers were correct in always stressing that this critical and relativizing characteristic is a necessary part of cognition ... To the degree that the knowledge gained from perception and inference, methodical inquiry and historical events, daily work and political struggle, meets the test of the available means of cognition, if it is the truth.[19]

At the deeper level of fundamental values, Marcuse adopted a historical aprioristic position, which was that on the basis of humanity's historical experience it is possible to extract values which are a priori 'correct'; that human life should be worth living, for example, should, he maintained, be self-evident to all rational human beings. Thus with respect to his definition of human essence and the question of why certain elements of humanity's experience should be 'remembered' and 'refined' and not others, and why only those 'religious and ethical ideal conceptions of a more just order of things be preserved', he admitted that an element of apriorism was at work — but one that took as its starting point the actual history of humanity:

> In truth, an a priori element is at work here, but one confirming the historicity of the concept of essence. It leads

back into history rather than out of it.[20]

Marcuse's concept of critical rationality — which is the cutting edge of his social theory — is undoubtedly also subversive of the relationship between social classes and revolution in that the rational goals of humanity are a sacred trust, a duty which can be forfeited by the social class that is its bearer in capitalist society — the proletariat. The position of the proletariat in capitalist society makes its particular interest the interest of all humanity; but this need not be the case, for there is only a historical and not a necessary link between the working class and the rational goals of the species. The consciousness of a class, for Marcuse, only had universal significance if it contained these goals. Thus while in the thirties he accepted Marx's reasons for characterising the proletariat as the revolutionary class, he nonetheless saw the proletariat's significance purely in terms of its being the necessary liberator of all humanity. Thus he wrote in an analysis of Hegel's discussion of universals:

> If the individual ... were nothing but a member of a particular class, race or nation, his claims could not reach beyond his particular group, and he would simply have to accept its standards.[21]

In this respect Marcuse, as a true child of the Enlightenment, held the belief that the divisions amongst individuals concealed a common nature and a common destiny; and therein lay the source of his growing ambivalence towards the revolutionary role of the proletariat.

This is probably a good point at which to examine Marcuse's analysis of the nature of his own social theory — which he referred to as critical theory, and not as marxism. The term critical theory seems to have been coined by Horkheimer in 1937, and it was preferred to the term marxism for two main reasons. Firstly, there was the factor of what we might term the 'closet marxism' of the Institute; a fear, which persisted from its earliest days, of alienating the academic world by an explicit commitment to marxism. Thus the planned *Institut für Marx-*

ismus became the *Institut für Sozialforschung*. This fear was reinforced by the Institute's move to the USA, as it was dependent on the temporary accommodation offered by Columbia University and the use of the term critical theory was partially determined by this fear (an early euphemism for their social theory had been 'materialism'). A second and more important reason was that the exponents of critical theory felt that the term 'marxism' would not adequately convey the specific nature of their theory. Although Marx and Engels were considered to be the founders of critical theory, this did not preclude criticism or development of their work nor the use of insights drawn from other schools of thought.

The use of the term 'critical' had two main sources. Firstly there was the negative concept of reality derived from dialectical philosophy, which we have already encountered, and its inherent criticism of the given. Secondly, however, there was Marx's critique of political economy. Let us now establish the relationship between the various elements of Marcuse's social theory: namely philosophy, the critique of political economy, and critical theory, starting first with the relationship between the last two of these.

According to Marcuse, Marx's critique of political economy represents the authentic method of analysis of a capitalist society. This method contains two crucial insights derived from Hegel. The first is that the correct method is one that follows the actual process of reality and not one that is arbitrarily imposed; and the second is that a negative totality cannot be known directly but only through its manifest forms, for although essence and appearance differ, essence only exists as appearance. The reality of capitalism can therefore only be known by a double abstraction: an initial, false abstraction contained in those categories of political economy which capitalism necessarily develops in order to know itself; and a second, true abstraction from the first:

> The commodity world is a 'falsified' and 'mystified' world, and its critical analysis must first follow the abstractions which make up this world, and must then take its departure

21

from these abstract relations in order to arrive at their real content.[22]

This method simultaneously reveals, indicts, and indicates possibilities. It reveals that 'economic relations are existential relations between men',[23] that the apparently objective relations of the capitalist mode of production are merely a particular form of existence that humanity has given itself whilst losing sight of this fact. It is thus an indictment, since it involves an implicit contrast between the actual and the rational:

> Objective facts come alive and enter an indictment of society. Economic realities exhibit their own inherent negativity ... Every fact is more than a mere fact; it is a negation and restriction of real possibilities. Wage labor is a fact, but at the same time is a restraint on free work that might satisfy human needs.[24]

This method indicates possibilities in two ways: it contrasts the essence with the enslaved condition of actual individuals, and shows the structural tendencies that will eventually destroy capitalism; in short, it shows both the subjective and the objective possibility — what should happen and what will happen. In the light of this, we can see why Marcuse cautioned against concentrating excessively on the work of the early Marx, for the philosophical critique that informed this early work is absorbed by the later economic categories which are more than merely philosophic or economic concepts. Both have been abolished in the hegelian sense of *Aufhebung*:

> Philosophy thus appears within the economic concepts of materialist theory, each of which is more than an economic concept of the sort employed by the academic discipline of economics. It is more due to the theory's claim to explain the totality of man and his world in terms of his social being. Yet it would be false on that account to reduce these concepts to philosophical ones. To the contrary, the philosophical contents relevant to the theory are to be educed from the economic structure. They refer to

conditions that, when forgotten, threaten the theory as a whole.[25]

Marcuse considered critical theory to be the heir to this revolutionary method, whose concern is to reveal the negativity in the given and the way in which negation can itself be negated. Whether this claim is spurious or not should become clearer once we have examined the relationship between philosophy and critical theory. We have already seen one relationship: critical theory abolishes philosophy in the hegelian sense. However, two other relationships exist, namely that philosophy, like any other mode of thought, can be subjected to the critical method Marx employed with political economy; and finally, that philosophy, insofar as it contains truth, will be actualised by practice via critical theory. We shall begin by examining the first of these two relationships.

Why, according to Marcuse, did Marx in his earliest work engage in a critique of philosophy? This was because the social, economic and political conditions in the Germany of his time were so backward (in relation to Britain and France) that German philosophy contained, albeit in an ideal realm, a more advanced object of study than the 'real' conditions themselves. Hegel's dialectic presented in an 'abstract logical' form the actual development of European society, which therefore served as an initial abstraction that could form the basis for a true abstraction (the real content). It was Marcuse's contention that European society in the 1930s had once more fallen behind its theoretical manifestations:

> In a different form, the situation confronting the theory of society in the nineteenth century is being repeated today. Once again real conditions fall beneath the general level of history ... The reflection cast by the truth of the future in the philosophy of the past provides indications of factors that point beyond today's anachronistic conditions.[26]

It was this activity, the critical analysis of systems of thought, particularly philosophy, that formed Marcuse's actual project during his period with the Institute. All his articles of this period (save one written at the very end of his Institute days[27]) consist largely of a vigorous if selective critique of the whole western tradition of philosophy, in an attempt to rescue forgotten values, expose error and reveal the essential as opposed to the apparent meaning of the elements of this tradition.

Philosophy, for Marcuse, could not be reduced to mere ideology. It can contain truths locked in a mystificatory form and it is the task of critical theory to extract and enshrine these lost dimensions. Thus, for example, the concern of philosophy with abstract universals is a mystified embodiment of universal human values that have become lost to the consciousness of much of humanity, values such as 'man is a rational being, that this being requires freedom, and that happiness is his highest good'.[28] Critical theory liberates the critique and the promise from the inadequate ideological shell of philosophy.

Critical theory also reveals the truth of 'untruth' in philosophy. Marcuse sought, for example, to reveal the real nature of what he termed 'positivism', namely the philosophy of understanding (*Verstand*). The protagonists of this ill-defined school included Hume, Comte and the logical positivists of the Vienna Circle. Their common principle and, in Marcuse's opinion, their cardinal error, is 'the ultimate authority of the fact',[29] whereby they fail to see facts as elements of a negative totality. The positivists adhere to an erroneous epistemology which assumes the existence of real, isolated monads (facts) which are independent of the knowing subject, whose knowledge of these objects in some mysterious way reflects them. Marcuse did not deny the existence of the objective world (no idealist he), but insisted that it can only be known through a process involving the interaction of subject and object. Reality can only be known through cognition and cognition inevitably involves evaluation, for an object is always an object-for-a-subject. For example, capitalism can be a beneficial economic system or a mechanism involving the degradation of the individual; it cannot be simply 'capitalism', and those who refuse to see the evaluation involved in cogni-

24

tion acquiesce in the current determination of the given. If the subject fails to determine the object self-consciously, the object will determine the subject. Positivism has forgotten the crucial fact of the subject's constitution of the world, first developed in German idealist philosophy:

> It has been the fundamental conviction of idealism that truth is not given to man from some external source but originates in the process of interaction between thought and reality, theory and practice. The function of thought was not merely to collect, comprehend and order facts, but also to contribute a quality that rendered such activity possible, a quality that was thus a priori to facts.[30]

Positivism is therefore epistemologically naive and potentially conservative in political terms. However, Marcuse argued that philosophical doctrines have to be evaluated in context. Although nineteenth-century and twentieth-century positivism is essentially regressive this was not the case with the seventeenth-century philosophical appeal to facts, which served as an important weapon against the theological world view of the declining feudal order. That doctrines change their function was an enduring belief in Marcuse's work.

Some doctrines, however, cannot be adapted indefinitely and become historically superfluous. Such is the case with liberalism, which was defined by Marcuse as:

> the social and economic theory of European capitalism in the period when the actual economic bearer of capitalism was the 'individual capitalist', the private entrepreneur in the literal sense.[31]

The fundamental basis of liberalism, in this interpretation, was a belief in the sanctity of private property which inextricably linked it to capitalism. According to Marcuse, European fascism in the 1920s and 1930s had its foundation in the monopoly capitalism that replaced the earlier mercantile and industrial capitalism; thus fascism took over the essential liberal belief in private property. Fascism and liberalism are therefore the appropriate ideologies of different stages of development of the same mode of production:

> The turn from the liberalist to the total-authoritarian state occurs within the framework of a single social order. With regard to the unity of this economic base, we can say it is liberalism that 'produces' the total-authoritarian state out of itself, as its own consummation at a more advanced stage of development. The total-authoritarian state brings with it the organization and theory of society that correspond to the monopolistic stage of capitalism.[32]

Paradoxically, fascist ideology contains a genuine critique of elements of liberalism. Reason is privatised in liberalism: the individual is only allowed to be rational as a private subject, for it is believed that the hidden hand of reason works through the 'free market'; and consequently, any collective rational construction of the whole is precluded. Similarly, liberalism proclaims the inner freedom of the individual to be higher than mere civil or social freedom, a clear rationalisation of the actual civil and social unfreedom that prevails in capitalist society. Both these elements are present in the general distinction in liberalism between state and society, state and individual, in which the latter is depoliticised in each case. The opposition of fascism to these elements is thus in this respect progressive:

> In consciously politicizing the concept of existence, and deprivatizing and deinternalizing ... the liberalist, idealist conception of man, the totalitarian view of the state represents progress.[33]

However, the 'progressive' elements of fascism become regressive, since they operate within the capitalist mode of production, for the genuine heir to the progressive elements of both liberal and totalitarian theory is critical theory and as such represents the synthesis of both liberalism and its antithesis.

Let us now turn to the third relationship between philosophy and critical theory. As already stated, philosophy is one refuge for truths that have been repelled by current organisations of society, thus philosophy cannot legitimately be abolished until its truth is realised in practice; in other words, until philosophy is actualised. Evident here is the influence of the Marx of the *Introduction to the Contribution to the Critique of Hegel's Philosophy of Law*: 'you cannot supersede philosophy without making it a reality'.[34] The truths of philosophy must be translated into real conditions, truths philosophy had retained long before the birth of critical theory:

> the philosophical construction of reason is replaced by the creation of a rational society. The philosophical ideals of a better world and true Being are incorporated into the practical aim of struggling mankind where they take on a human form.[35]

In the light of the above, what credence are we to give to Marcuse's claim that his work (and that of his Institute colleagues) represented a creative development of Marx's critique of political economy? It seems clear that Marcuse's concerns differed in emphasis from those of Marx, for whereas Marx was principally concerned with revealing structural tendencies in capitalism, Marcuse sought to de-mystify consciousness. Once more we can see the influence of the early Marx, who in a letter to Ruge in 1843 called for a 'critical philosophy' that would enable people to see through their mystified consciousness:

> Our programme must be: the reform of consciousness ... by analysing mystical consciousness obscure to itself ... It will then become plain that the world has long dreamed of something of which it needs only to become conscious for it to possess it in reality.[36]

Marx concluded this letter with a definition of the aim of his journal, the *Deutsch-Französische Jahrbücher* — an aim which could appropriately be applied to the Institute's journal — *Zeitschrift für Sozialforschung*:

We are therefore in a position to sum up the credo of our journal in a single word: the self-clarification (critical philosophy) of the struggles and wishes of the age.[37]

Marcuse, like Horkheimer and Adorno, was in fact largely uninterested in economics — an understandable but not excusable lacuna, in that at first Marx had also not been interested in such matters, though he later realised that they were crucial to an adequate social theory. It should however be noted that at the very end of his period with the Institute (see chapter 3), and especially after his departure from that body, Marcuse began to pay more attention to analysing structural determination.

Before examining the relationship between critical theory and practice, we must first complete our picture of the sort of functions subsumed under the concept of critical theory. Critical theory not only indicts but also reveals possibilities therefore it contains both an ethical and an analytical component. However, it has a third function, which we might term 'anticipation', based upon the faculty of imagination; for when Marcuse said that 'the abyss between rational and present reality cannot be bridged by conceptual thought',[38] he was doing more than re-stating the marxist commonplace enshrined in the last 'Thesis on Feuerbach', for he in fact insisted on the necessity of non-conceptual cognition in critical theory. The concept of phantasy lies at the centre of this belief: 'In order to retain what is not yet present as a goal in the present, phantasy is required.'[39] Once more Marcuse developed a concept whose pedigree can be traced back through the western tradition of philosophy to Aristotle. The faculty of imagination enables one to transcend the given by cognitively creating the future which will then serve as a spur to its practical realisation. Phantasy is the crucial cognitive link with the future.

Great art, Marcuse believed, has been one of the major vehicles for these flights of phantasy, for it retains a vision of a better world in the teeth of its actual betrayal. Schiller's aesthetic theory seems to have influenced Marcuse greatly in this respect. Long before he met Adorno, who was to influence him profoundly in aesthetic matters, he had engrossed himself in a study of Schiller, and his first publication (1925) was a bibliography of Schiller. In a 1937 essay, Marcuse acknowledged his debt to this thinker as regards the relationship between art and truth. Speaking of one of Schiller's poems, he stated:

> In his poem 'Die Künstler' ... he expresses the relationship between the established and the coming culture in the lines: 'What we have here perceived as beauty / We shall one day encounter as truth'.[40]

In Schiller's *On the Aesthetic Education of Man* we can see two ideas which anticipated Marcuse's analysis of the revolutionary potential of art; the first is that art provides a source of critical images which enable individuals to engage in political activity, and the second is that art has autonomy even *vis-à-vis* its creator.[41] With regard to the first of these ideas Marcuse considered art to be both anticipatory and critical, in that albeit momentarily it substitutes a better reality for the one currently experienced:

> There is an element of earthly delight in the works of great bourgeois art ... the individual enjoys beauty, goodness, splendor, peace and victorious joy ... he experiences liberation ... reification is transpierced in private ... The world appears as what it is behind the commodity form: a landscape is really a landscape, a man is really a man, a thing is really a thing.[42]

These features of art exist regardless of, and often despite the actual political motives (if any) of the artist: for art, like philosophy, cannot be reduced to mere ideology. Reactionary artists can and do produce oeuvres which possess truth value. Marcuse thereby adopted a position which was violently disputed by many on the left, for it owed more to the romantic notions of the genius harnessing the universal than it did to traditions which considered that the explicit political orientation of the form, of its content and of its creator were of paramount importance. Great art is contrasted with the ersatz products of mass culture, which are in no sense anticipatory or critical, as they are, in Horkheimer's words, 'nothing but popular tonics'.[43] However, Marcuse did not advocate popular appropriation of 'great art', and this apparently paradoxical position was derived from his conviction that the latter has an 'affirmative' quality.

Marcuse defined affirmative culture as:

> that culture of the bourgeois epoch which led in the course of its own development to the segregation from civilization of the mental and spiritual world as an independent realm of value that is also considered superior to civilization.[44]

The principal function of this affirmative culture is to make the lot of the individual tolerable in a world in which the capitalist mode of production ensures that only a very few can ever achieve even a semblance of happiness. It offers people satisfaction in an ideal realm, thus simultaneously affirming and concealing the actual inhuman organisation of society:

> To the need of the isolated individual it responds with general humanity, to bodily misery with the beauty of the soul, to external bondage with internal freedom, to brutal egoism with the duty of the realm of virtue.[45]

The call of the left for the proletariat to 'take over' the artistic heritage of the past was consequently considered by Marcuse to be dangerous in that it merely exposes that class to yet another ideological reinforcement of the bourgeoisie. In an explicit attack on the cultural policy of the SPD in general and on the work of Karl Kautsky in particular, he argued that the policy of 'art for the masses' 'can mean nothing other than winning the masses to the social order that is affirmed by the "entire culture" '.[46] Great art should not be diffused but abolished as beauty and enjoyment are taken out of the concert halls and museums and fully socialised in post-class society, where 'perhaps art as such will have no objects'.[47]

This inevitably brings us to the issue of the relationship between critical theory and political practice. The first point to be made is that Marcuse eschewed any notion of determinism with regard to the transition between capitalism and socialism, a position based upon a philosophical and an empirical argument. With regard to the former it is necessary to examine his analysis of the hegelian and marxist dialectic.

As I have stated previously, Marcuse maintained that Marx and Hegel both considered reality to be a 'negative totality', but he sided with Marx against Hegel as to the nature of this totality, for whilst Hegel's totality was essentially metaphysical, in that it concerned the process of the development of Being, Marx's totality was a process rooted in actual human history. For Marx:

> the negativity of reality becomes a *historical* condition which cannot be hypostatized as a metaphysical state of affairs. In other words, it becomes a social condition, associated with a particular historical form of society.[48]

Hegel had erroneously generalised the abstract, logical form of the development of a particular stage of human history — class society or pre-history. That was why he saw the dialectical process as law-determined: for the dialectic reflects the actual law-determined movement of class society. Movement in such societies is blind, unconscious and completely lacking in self-conscious control. For this reason, Marcuse believed it is permissible to talk of capitalism as a determined mode of production. However it is not permissible to speak of any such determination as far as the transition to socialism is concerned, because the essence of such a transition is that individuals take conscious control of their society. An unconscious transition to socialism is a contradiction in terms, for socialism can only emerge as the creation of free subjects: 'There can be no blind necessity in the tendencies that terminate in a free and self-conscious society.'[49] The mode of existence which will characterise socialism needs to be reflected in the forces struggling to usher it in. A revolution therefore requires objective conditions, the main ones being 'a certain attained level of material and intellectual culture', 'a self-conscious and organized working class on an international scale', and 'acute class struggle'; but: 'these become revolutionary conditions, however, only if seized upon and directed by a conscious activity that has in mind the socialist goal.'[50]

Marx himself was upbraided in *Reason and Revolution* for making the unwarranted asssumption 'that the same mechanisms that bring about the concentration and centralisation of capital also produce the "socialization of labor" '.[51] It was implied that Marx, contrary to the spirit of his theory, succumbed at times to determinism with regard to the transition between capitalism and socialism. What Marcuse failed to discuss is that insofar as there is a determinist element in Marx it is due to the influence of Hegel. Marx never liberated himself totally from Hegel's teleological vision, and one does sense at times that for Marx, the proletariat fulfilled the same function as the world historical individuals did for Hegel — namely, as an agent of a higher necessity, an agent of a necessary task where 'necessary' does not simply mean desirable but inevitable. The hegelian vision — and even the hegelian terminology — linger on in *Capital*, where in Chapter XXXII of *Capital I*, for example, Marx wrote: 'Capitalist production begets, with the inexorability of a law of Nature, its own negation. It is the negation of negation.'[52] Marcuse was however quite right to point out that insofar as this is determinism, it is incompatible with Marx's theory. For Marx himself never argued that the transition to socialism was an unconscious process, for the proletariat would only fulfil its historical task once it became conscious of it. Marcuse's main objection to Marx's account of the transition was essentially empirical, in that Marx believed that capitalism would necessarily radicalise the proletariat; Marcuse disagreed, for although he accepted that capitalism would inevitably perish by virtue of the laws Marx had discovered, he did not accept that socialism would necessarily result.

We term this argument 'empirical' because it emerged from Marcuse's growing pessimism about the revolutionary potential of the proletariat. The triumphs of fascism, the development of the Spanish Civil War and the Moscow Show Trials all pointed to one pessimistic conclusion, which he voiced in 1934 before some of the above had even happened, namely that 'today the fate of the labor movement ... is clouded with uncertainty'.[53] The revolutionary class appeared to be unable to develop the necessary class consciousness for revolutionary activity, which raised the possibility that capitalism might collapse into barbarism and not into socialism. Critical theory, however, retains the lost goal of classless society and this legitimises criticism of the proletariat itself since its actual consciousness does not contain the vital universal component:

> In view of the possibility of a happier real state of humanity the interest of the individual is no longer an ultimate datum ... His factual, immediate interest is not in itself his true interest.[54]

Revolution is dependent to a far greater degree than ever before on that 'conscious activity that has in mind the socialist goal', and it is to Marcuse's development of this idea that we will now turn.

We are immediately confronted by a problem. For Marcuse's work in the thirties was remarkably lacking in strategic and tactical analysis: and this reflected not only the alien conditions of his American exile, but the pessimism to which I have already referred.

It seems clear that Marcuse did not rule out the possibility that the 'conscious element' in a revolution could be provided by a revolutionary party. In a 1936 article on authority, he looked favourably upon what he termed Engel's 'positive concept of authority', which embraced the authority exercised by the leadership of a revolutionary party:

> Engels holds up another decisive function of genuine authority as an objection against the anti-authoritarian: the role of leadership and the leading party in the revolution ... Revolutionary subordination in one's own ranks

and revolutionary authority towards the class enemy are necessary prerequisites in the struggle for the future organization of society.[55]

Marcuse also considered that Lenin's theory of the party enshrined a positive concept of authority and that it provided a 'conscious' moment to the revolution by injecting class political consciousness into the proletariat from without and by guiding the development of the revolution. He explicitly sided with Lenin against the rival conceptions of anarchism and spontaneous revolution; with regard to Lenin's work, he concluded:

> From the importance of the conscious element there emerges the necessity for a strict, centralist organization with a proven and schooled leadership at its head.[56]

For a number of reasons, however, we must beware of making a glib characterisation of Marcuse as a leninist in considering his revolutionary strategy: firstly, Marcuse was always aware of the specificity of revolutionary situations, and consequently highly critical of any attempt to fetishise organisational forms. Thus, although Lenin's model is commended, there is no suggestion that it is universally applicable. Secondly, Marcuse was mindful of the tendency of rational authority to turn into irrational authoritarianism as the mode of organisation loses its original specific function and develops general and illegitimate functions which relate to the mere continuation of its own existence. When this happens — and Marcuse made this clear in his 1936 article — the leninist avant-garde becomes as illegitimate as the fascist elites:

> Direct lines of development have been drawn from Sorel's concept of social élites, to both the proletarian 'avant-garde' of Leninism and to the élite 'leaders' of Fascism. Freed from the connection with a clear economic base and elevated into a 'moral' sphere, the conception of the élite tends towards formalistic authoritarianism.[57]

Finally, Marcuse's mentor and close collaborator in this period, Max Horkheimer, replaced the leninist dualism of party and class with a tripartite distinction between critical theorists, party and class:

> The course of the conflict between the advanced sectors of the class and the individuals who speak out the truth concerning it, as well as of the conflict between the most advanced sectors with their theoreticians and the rest of the class, is to be understood as a process of interactions in which awareness comes to flower along with its liberating but also its aggressive forces which incite while also requiring discipline.[58]

Horkheimer conceived of these three elements as a 'dynamic' unity; however, the modus operandi of this unity is nowhere described in detail. In short, the evidence available at present is too scanty to admit of a definitive answer to the question of Marcuse's 'leninism' in this period and therefore we must await the findings of some future biographer who has access to Marcuse's private papers.

Deeply embedded in critical theory is a belief in the hazardousness of prediction. Marcuse did not rule out prediction in the context of class society since, as we saw earlier, he asserted that capitalism will inevitably destroy itself; in *Reason and Revolution*, he cited the work of Henryk Grossman as a supplementary authority to Marx on this issue,[59] and described Grossman nearly forty years later as 'the most orthodox of all the Marxist economists I have ever met — he predicted the collapse of Capitalism for a specific year!'.[60] However, Grossman was rather out on a limb at the Institute and it was the work of Frederick Pollock — who 'argued that there was no compelling internal economic reasons why Capitalism should collapse'[61] — which more accurately reflected the stance of the Institute on this matter. If in this respect Marcuse was willing to engage in prediction this, as we have again seen, did not extend to an assertion of the inevitability of socialism. Socialism was not inevitable but desirable, a projected embodiment of universal values which was to guide political activity. For Marcuse, predictions had only provisional value and their empirical falsification in no way falsified critical theory as the theory, being founded upon a concern with the happiness of humanity, did not admit of falsification. The falsification of predictions merely served to enrich the theory by highlighting false assumptions and new developments:

> What if the development outlined by the theory does not occur? What if the forces that were to bring about the transformation are suppressed and appear to be defeated? Little as the theory's truth is thereby contradicted, it nevertheless appears then in a new light which illuminates new aspects and elements of its object.[62]

According to Horkheimer, all that remains constant in capitalism is an 'empirical' proposition and evaluation — that capitalism is class-based and exploitative;[63] within these parameters, however, mutation is limitless.

If it is hazardous to formulate predictions with regard to class society it is the more so with regard to post-class society. The distinction Marx drew in his early work between the pre-history of humanity in class society and humanity's actual history in communism is one that exercised a particular fascination for Marcuse, for it asserted that the nature of communist existence was qualitatively different; and although communist existence can be partially anticipated in phantasy, it will be of such a richness that it will preclude any comprehensive anticipation by individuals in class society. This can legitimately be termed the utopian strain in Marcuse's work — a vision of limitless possibilities for human fulfilment, the communist vision of the Marx of the *Economic and Philosophical Manuscripts*:

> it is the genuine resolution of the conflict between man and nature and between man and man — the true resolution of the strife between existence and essence, between

objectification and self-confirmation, between freedom and necessity, between the individual and the species. Communism is the riddle of history solved and it knows itself to be the solution.[64]

For Marcuse, even the idea of reason did not convey the full impact of the difference between present and rational reality; thus in *Reason and Revolution* he stated that for critical theory 'The idea of reason has been superseded by the idea of happiness'[65] and anticipated his 1950s concept of the 'rationality of gratification' — the convergence of reason and happiness.

The principal danger in this utopian strain of thought is that it magnifies the gap between pre- and post-class society and thereby renders the transition from one to the other a seemingly impossible task, in that the selling of newspapers and participation in industrial action, for example, will seem pathetically inadequate to those seeking to solve the riddle of history. The vision can thus act like Medusa's head and freeze individuals into total immobility — cases in point being Horkheimer and Adorno, for whom the vision was so sublime and the human material so base that they retreated from politics into total privatisation. In the case of Marcuse, this sense of the qualitative leap involved in the transition to socialism led him at times to underestimate the revolutionary potential of ordinary working people and to overestimate that of marginal groups.

Yet as we have seen there was also, in Marcuse's thought, an anti-utopian element: the inevitability of the realm of necessity, the unhappiness caused by the mutability of the world, the limits of technical possibility, are all flies in the communist ointment. Also the given, even the given of communism, can never be self-justifying — it has to satisfy the tribunal of critical rationality: 'Theory will preserve the truth even if revolutionary practice deviates from its proper path. Practice follows the truth not vice versa'.[66] The tension between subject and object can never be dispensed with.

3. Eros

The 1940s witnessed the parting of Marcuse's way from that of his Institute colleagues, Horkheimer and Adorno. This parting was two-fold: on the one hand there came a physical separation, the result of his service with the US government; and on the other, a divergence of interests and perspectives which, whilst we may acknowledge Marcuse's continuing intellectual debt to these thinkers, makes it legitimate for us to consider him as an independent thinker, distinct from the Frankfurt School after the early forties.

It is perhaps difficult today to imagine the tremendous culture-shock experienced by Marcuse and the other members of the Institute when they moved from Weimar Germany to New Deal America. These individuals were to a large extent repelled by the culture of their new home. Adorno, writing in the 1960s, recalled:

> I still remember the shock that a housemaid, an emigrant like ourselves, gave me during our first few days in New York when she, the daughter of a so-called good home, explained: 'People in my town used to go to the symphony, now they go to Radio City'. In no way did I want to be like her. Even if I had wanted to I wouldn't have been capable of it. By nature and personal history, I was unsuitable for 'adjustment' in intellectual matters.[1]

This feeling was common to that entire generation of exiled central European intellectuals. Brecht, for example:

> On thinking about Hell I gather
> My brother Shelley found it was a place

Much like the city of London. I
Who live in Los Angeles and not in London
Find, on thinking about Hell, that it must be
Still more like Los Angeles.[2]

Marcuse was no different in this respect, and although the full
venom of his feelings about American culture did not emerge
until his writings of the early 1960s one can sense his antipathy
in the way he described an average American car journey in
1941:

A man who travels by automobile to a distant place
chooses his route from the highway maps. Towns, lakes
and mountains appear as obstacles to be bypassed. The
countryside is shaped and organised by the highway: what
one finds en route is a byproduct or annexe of the
highway. Numerous signs and posters tell the traveller
what to do and think; they even request his attention to the
beauties of nature or the hallmarks of history ... conve-
nient parking spaces have been constructed where the
broadest and most surprising view is open. Giant adver-
tisements tell him where to stop and find the pause that
refreshes.[3]

Marcuse considered his work for US Intelligence as part of
the anti-fascist struggle which was the priority of the day, and
which necessarily involved victory in the world war. In 1941,
and in what was to be his last article until very much later in the
decade, Marcuse wrote:

Fascism has transformed economic expansion into the
military conquest of whole continents. In this situation,
the restoration of society to its own right, and the
maintenance of individual freedom have become directly
political questions, their solution depending on the out-
come of the international struggle.[4]

He did, however, remain in government service after the war
had finished — in fact, until 1951; this prolongation was partly

the result of the lengthy illness of his wife, who died in that year. He was thus 53 when he left the State Department and, under its sponsorship, became a Senior Fellow in the Russian Institute and special lecturer at Columbia University. This was the first of a couple of temporary academic appointments he accepted before 1954, when he obtained the post at Brandeis University in which he was to remain for 11 years. His students of this period recall how this committed man stood out from the native 'liberal' academic establishment, whose profession of 'objectivity' he rightly considered to be a joke in rather bad taste. One such student, David Kettler, recalled his initial encounter with Marcuse in 1951:

> We delighted in the fact that Kingsley Davis taught a Sociology course entitled 'Theories of Social Change' while Marcuse named his course starkly 'The Theory of Social Change'.[5]

Marcuse's teaching manner, if we consider his social theory and his background in the magisterial traditions of German education, must have appeared to students inured to Anglo-American traditions to verge on the intolerant. Kettler, again:

> Marcuse was asked to comment on theories of history which contend that history repeats itself; he leaned across the lectern, then asked in definitive astonishment, 'Do you really think it does?' and proceeded with his lecture.[6]

Although in an interview many years later Marcuse insisted that one 'must subtract'[7] the years 1940 to 1950 from his intellectual career, this period saw Marcuse engaged, amongst other matters, in an intensive study of the work of Freud, a thinker to whom he had first been seriously directed by Max Horkheimer back in the 1930s. An interest in psychology was one of the major innovations Horkheimer introduced to the Institute on his assumption of its directorship; and psychology — or rather, an adequate psychology for both himself and his colleagues, as Marcuse himself explained[8] — meant the work of

Freud. The main focus of the Institute's psychological work was an analysis of the psychic factors involved in the genesis of ideology and of ideological behaviour, this project being under the broad guidance of Erich Fromm. According to Fromm, freudian psychoanalysis was a materialist psychology which facilitated the revelation of those hidden instinctual drives which motivated human behaviour and which became expressed in the form of ideologies.[9] Marcuse was not really involved in the psychological concerns of the Institute in this period of the 1930s, for although he shared the freudian perspectives of his colleagues his main focus of attention was on the western tradition of philosophy (it is significant that in the Institute's psychological work on authority and the family, of 1936, he contributed a history of the philosophical expression of the concept of authority and a similar history of its sociological expression), and he has revealed since that he considered the Institute's work in the 1930s to be 'too psychological'.[10] This degree of distance enabled Marcuse to develop an area neglected by his colleagues, an area that anticipated his later work in *Eros and Civilization*, namely the revolutionary nature of sexuality.

Capitalist society, for Marcuse, inevitably induced sexual repression since its continued existence required the postponement of gratification in the workplace, for most work in such a society is inherently unpleasurable. One dimension of the much vaunted freedom of capitalism is thus the freedom to repress one's basic drives — except for severely circumscribed periods, after work:

> Bourgeois society has liberated individuals, but as persons who are to keep themselves in check. From the beginning the prohibition of pleasure was a condition of freedom.[11]

Hedonistic philosophies have therefore contained a radical and progressive element in that, root and branch, they oppose this devaluation of pleasure:

> By identifying happiness with pleasure, they were demanding that man's sensual and sensuous potentialities and

needs, too, should find satisfaction ... Insofar as the materialistic protest of hedonism preserves an otherwise proscribed element of human liberation, it is linked with the interest of critical theory.[12]

In a conception more akin to the work of Wilhelm Reich than to that of Fromm and the Institute, Marcuse saw in sexuality a force so powerful that it had the potential to ultimately destroy the repressive work ethic which sustained capitalism:

The unpurified, unrationalized release of sexual relationships would be the strongest release of enjoyment as such and the total devaluation of labor for its own sake. No human being could tolerate the tension between labor as valuable in itself and the freedom of enjoyment. The dreariness and injustice of work conditions would penetrate explosively the consciousness of individuals and make impossible their peaceful subordination to the social system of the bourgeois world.[13]

During this period, he did not develop this insight and its development did not in fact take place until *Eros and Civilization*, over 15 years later. Before this work, Marcuse returned once more to the issue of sexuality in a review article of Sartre's *Being and Nothingness* in 1948, where, in a generally hostile critique, he was favourably disposed towards Sartre's concept of the '*attitude désirante*' which is essentially sexual desire. In sexual desire, according to Sartre, one ceases to be a manipulating subject and becomes instead an object, aware of oneself as a sensual body. Thus one becomes 'pervaded by the mere facticity (of one's existence as body), to cease fleeing from it, and to glide into a passive ascent to desire'.[14] Other individuals too are seen purely as sensual objects: relationships are structured purely on the basis of the pleasure principle rather than the dehumanising principles which normally characterise relationships in a capitalist society. Thus, paradoxically, what is in effect the height of reification becomes the ground for liberation:

Enslavement and repression are cancelled ... in the sphere of the 'corps vécu comme chair', the 'trame d'inertie' ... Reification itself turns into liberation.[15]

As early as 1937, Marcuse had highlighted this paradox of total reification, the nature of which could be seen in certain marginal cultural manifestations:

When the body has completely become an object, a beautiful thing, it can foreshadow a new happiness. In suffering the most extreme reification man triumphs over reification. The artistry of the beautiful body, its effortless agility and relaxation, which can be displayed today only in the circus, vaudeville, and burlesque, herald the joy to which men will attain ...[16]

His integration of these insights into the comprehensive system outlined in *Eros and Civilization* was essentially a response to what he perceived as crucial historical developments, particularly the collapse of revolutionary activity in the west and the degeneration of the Soviet Union, developments he broadly defined in a 1954 epilogue to *Reason and Revolution* as the retreat of freedom:

Freedom is on the retreat — in the realm of thought as well as in that of society. Neither the hegelian nor the marxian idea of Reason have come closer to realization; neither the development of the Spirit nor that of the Revolution took the form envisaged by dialectical theory.[17]

One of the principal functions of *Eros and Civilization* was to explain why this was so by using the psychoanalytic insights of Freud. In this respect, Marcuse was belatedly engaging in the same type of activity as his former Institute colleagues. It seemed to him that the wholesale collapse of revolutionary hopes could not be totally explained by simply referring to the work of Marx and Engels which, while fundamentally sound, nonetheless lacked an essential psychological dimension. He hypothesised that there was a deep instinctual element in individuals which led them historically to betray their own revolutionary activity. As he wrote in *Eros and Civilization*:

> In every revolution, there seems to have been a historical moment when the struggle against domination might have been victorious — but the moment passed. An element of self-defeat seems to be involved in this dynamic ... In this sense, every revolution has also been a betrayed revolution.[18]

Using the 9th Thermidor (the day that marked the end of the jacobin stage of the French Revolution and the beginning of the triumph of the counter-revolution) as a symbol for this process, he speculated in a lecture given in 1956 that 'alongside the socio-historical Thermidor ... there is ... also a psychic Thermidor'.[19] To understand this speculation it is necessary to examine the nature of Marcuse's appropriation of Freud.

Before doing so it should be mentioned that Marcuse accepted without question the validity of Freud's clinical findings, and granted them a scientific status which is on a par with that of Marx's findings in *Capital*; he made no attempt to analyse the clinical work of Freud from a historical materialist standpoint. Marcuse was intent on shaking our faith in some of the social conclusions Freud drew from his findings yet expected us to take on trust that these findings were valid.

Marcuse considered that Freud's theory of human instincts was central to the latter writer's work, the development of which he periodised according to the changes in this theory; thus there is an initial dualism of sex versus self-preservation, an intermediate period where all-pervasive (narcissistic) libido is assumed, and a final reformulated dualism of life instinct (Eros) and the death instinct. Marcuse was principally concerned with the last of these three periods — Freud's work after 1920. He adopted wholesale Freud's tripartite division of the personality into id, ego and superego.

Following Freud, he defined the id in terms of the layers of human mental structure as:

the fundamental, oldest, and largest layer ... the domain of the unconscious, of the primary instincts ... all it strives for is satisfaction of its instinctual needs, in accordance with the pleasure principle.[20]

This is the layer of the human psyche that seeks pure gratification, pure pleasure, the layer which is the source of the life instinct (Eros). However in a hostile environment the id's drive for total satisfaction endangers the very existence of the human organism, so a part of the id develops into the ego to protect the id from itself and thus replaces the pleasure principle with the reality principle. Marcuse agreed with Freud that this process of instinctual repression is a desideratum of any conceivable society but, unlike Freud, he refused to equate the reality principle of contemporary society with civilisation itself and instead posited a plurality of reality principles both historically and with respect to future possibility. He pejoratively termed the current reality principle the 'performance principle' in that 'under its rule society is stratified according to the competitive economic performance of its members'.[21] Reality principles are to be judged in terms of the amount of instinctual repression they enforce over and above the repression required for the simple preservation of the species — the degree to which 'surplus repression' is enforced beyond what is necessitated by 'basic repression'.[22] This can operate as a fundamental criterion because all forms of exploitation in a given society are ultimately dependent on this surplus instinctual repression.

Marcuse used the superego in his investigation of the 'psychic Thermidor' for, in short, the superego is the principal abortive mechanism deployed against the revolutionary impulse. The superego acts as an automatic reflex against gratification and perpetuates, by means of self-restraint in the individual, restrictions which were originally the product of external constraints — the parents, and other social institutions. Its role as the individual's conscience thus conceals its further function as the repository of the dominant values of society; in the case of a capitalist society the superego will inevitably reflect, albeit in varying degrees, the interests of the dominant economic class. Any attempt to revolt against these values results in the superego inducing guilt, an emotion whose power, first manifested at the individual level in the Oedipus Complex, is derived from a fundamental identification with the tyrant and thus 'the human objects of domination reproduce their own repression'.[23] The source of guilt cannot be adequately explained simply in terms of the life of the individual (ontogenesis) since it requires crucial supplementary explanation derived from the historical experience of the species (phylogenesis).

It is at this point in Marcuse's argument that the scattered insights of the thirties and forties are integrated into a more comprehensive framework. The dominant interests of capitalism require intense instinctual repression for their mode of production to be perpetuated — particularly sexual repression considering the explosive anti-labour potential of that drive. The sexual drives suffer the temporal restriction of the performance principle in that they are confined to severely limited after-work periods; and even then, the leisure industry keeps individuals from exploring their erotic possibilities if they are not already too tired to be interested in such exploration. This temporal restriction is supplemented by spatial restriction, as sexuality retreats into the so-called 'specialised sexual organs'. Thus 'the libido becomes concentrated in one part of the body, leaving most of the rest for use as the instrument of labor'.[24]

Marcuse's concepts of 'the performance principle' and 'surplus repression' clearly introduced a marxist perspective into his reading of Freud and operated as a critique of the latter's tendency to reduce the historically mutable to the biologically immutable. However, Marcuse was so concerned to show that Freud's biological concepts themselves contained a social component that he at times underestimated both the genuinely ahistorical tendencies in that writer's work and the extent of his own 'correction' of Freud. Thus, for example, after criticising the neo-freudian revisionists' (Fromm, Horney, Sullivan, and

Thompson) cultural and environmental 'correction' of Freud, he added:

> In contrast to the revisionists I believe that Freud's theory is in its very substance 'sociological' and that no new cultural or sociological orientation is needed.[25]

Marcuse's insistence on the implicit 'sociological' element in Freud's work was derived from his belief that the post-1920 works of this thinker, in their dualism of life instinct and death instinct, contained crucial insights into the history and prospects of humanity. As a result of that belief he took on board the very same late-freudian metapsychology that marxists had traditionally found so indigestible. This included the concept which above all others stuck in historical materialist craws — the death instinct.

The death instinct, which was first formulated in Freud's 1920 work *Beyond the Pleasure Principle*, lacks obvious appeal to marxists given its underlying assumption of a regressive human drive towards a tensionless, inorganic state. Fromm, writing for the Institute of Social Research in the 1930s, criticised this concept as a highly speculative and unwarranted amalgam of biology and psychology and compared it most unfavourably with Freud's early instinctual dualism of sex/self preservation, which 'saw the instincts primarily as wishing, desiring, and serving man's striving for life',[26] and which consequently (though Fromm did not spell this out) lent itself much more readily to marxist appropriation. Marcuse's move away from the Institute's position on this issue was motivated by his belief that Freud's early instinctual dualism could not explain *la condition humaine* adequately; as we shall see later, the death instinct was to play a part in Marcuse's phylogenetic account of the psychic Thermidor.

One feature of contemporary human civilisation in particular seemed to be explained by the death instinct — the tremendous build-up of human destructiveness as witnessed by the world war, atom bombs and, above all else, the extermination of six million Jews. Auschwitz, as a symbol of humanity's potential for destruction, was to recur throughout Marcuse's remaining works and the events of the holocaust revealed a dimension of human behaviour that his previous work had not appreciated. Thus, for example, in a 1965 foreword to a collection consisting mostly of his writings of the 1930s, Marcuse wrote: 'That most of this was written before Auschwitz deeply separates it from the present'.[27] Adorno also: 'To write poetry after Auschwitz is barbaric'.[28] In Marcuse's opinion, any adequate explanation of such events called for the use of Freud's theory of the relationship between the life instinct and the death instinct.

The death instinct (which following Freud he termed Thanatos) is in a complex relationship with the life instinct (Eros). Although derived from a common instinctual nature Eros and Thanatos become differentiated as antagonists: the former seeks to sustain life, the latter to destroy it. At both the ontogenetic and phylogenetic level Thanatos has tended to enforce repression and domination. At the ontogenetic level the superego is thoroughly permeated by Thanatos in that it uses a modification of the death instinct, the instinct for destruction, to split the personality by pitting the ego against the id. This is another way of saying that the death instinct enables surplus repression to be exacted. As Marcuse commented, 'Conscience, the most cherished moral agency of the civilized individual emerges as permeated with the death instinct.'[29] This surplus repression therefore not only results in the psychic Thermidor but also in a build-up of the death instinct in the superego — a great dam which under certain circumstances can burst out into an awesome wave of destructiveness.

The repression of the life instinct by the death instinct in the individual is not simply mirrored but actually determined by the same process at the phylogenetic level. To argue this Marcuse used Freud's description and analysis of the primal horde in *Moses and Monotheism*: not as an actual, historical account (for he accepted that it cannot be verified at that level), but as a heuristic device to explain the origins of what is known. At the beginning of human history, in Marcuse's account, the primal horde was ruled by a despotic tyrant who monopolised the supreme pleasure (the women) and who forced his sons to renounce pleasure, thus 'freeing' them to engage in the non-gratifying labour required for the preservation of the horde. Envy and hatred built up until the sons rose up and killed the father. This was the first historic act of liberation, but it was followed by the first 'psychic Thermidor', for the father, although a tyrant, was also the vital power required to enforce the necessary libidinal repression to ensure the production and reproduction of the means of existence; therefore his killing induced guilt in the sons:

> The rebellion against the father is rebellion against biologically justified authority; his assassination destroys the order which has preserved the life of the group. The rebels have committed a crime against the whole and thereby also against themselves. They are guilty before the others and before themselves, and they must repent.[30]

The father is consequently deified as a god and internalised as taboo/morality. Tyranny is reimposed and the revolution betrayed. Using Otto Rank's term a 'biological sense of guilt' Marcuse, following Freud, argued that a transhistorical burden of guilt reproduces repression in each new generation — a guilt which cannot be justified either in terms of the individual's actual transgressions or in terms of being a necessary condition for the survival of the species:

> [The individual's] autonomous personality appears as the frozen manifestation of the general repression of mankind ... psychology ... bares the sub-individual and pre-individual factors which (largely unconscious to the ego) actually make the individual: it reveals the power of the universal in and over the individuals.[31]

This is the psychic equivalent of what Marcuse had seen in *Reason and Revolution* as the blind dialectic governing class society. Individuals are still determined by these archaic impulses because they have not yet gained control of their own lives; they are still the objects of history and not yet its self-conscious subjects.

The guilt so experienced results in a profound fear of revolution which, if it is engaged in at all, leads to the eventual reimposition of domination. The historical dynamic of domination-liberation-domination has characterised all human history to date and has supplemented the great panoply of external controls which sustain oppressive organisations of society with self-control:

> ever since the first, prehistoric restoration of domination following the first rebellion, suppression from without has been supported by repression from within: the unfree individual introjects his masters and their commands into his own mental apparatus. The struggle against freedom reproduces itself in the psyche of man, as the self-repression of the repressed individual, and his self-repression in turn sustains his masters and their institutions.[32]

Engels, in a letter to Mehring of 14 July 1893, made his well-known remarks concerning the relationship between consciousness and its determinants, acknowledging his and Marx's neglect of detailed analysis of the nature of consciousness as opposed to its economic roots, and developing the notion of the interaction between superstructure and base where:

> once an historic element has been brought into the world by other, ultimately economic causes, it reacts, and can react on its environment and even on the causes that have given rise to it.[33]

Marcuse's notion of a transhistorical burden of guilt inhibiting the revolutionary impulse represents an extreme (and some might say unjustified) development of this notion of interaction, since it credits a psychic factor with causal power far greater than that of economic, social or political factors. It can be contrasted with Trotsky's account of the degeneration of the Soviet Union where despite being aware of the importance of psychic factors such as the degree of anti-semitism in the Russian masses, he at no point granted to unconscious motivation of this sort the causal power attributed to it by Marcuse. The betrayal of the Soviet revolution was not to be explained in terms of the unconscious dispositions of its participants but in terms of the inevitable problems associated with staging a revolution on an inadequate material base, an inadequacy assured by the absence of a world revolution. Thus, for example, the genesis of the Soviet bureaucracy is explained in terms of scarcity creating disorder and the response to this — the forces of order:

> The basis of bureaucratic rule is the poverty of society in objects of consumption, with the resulting struggle of each against all. When there is enough goods in a store, the purchasers can come whenever they want to. When there is little goods, the purchasers are compelled to stand in line. When the lines are very long it is necessary to appoint a policeman to keep order. Such is the starting point of the power of the Soviet bureaucracy.[34]

Marcuse's appropriation of freudian categories in general, and the notion of the archaic heritage of guilt in particular, represents a further development of the concept of human essence. Whilst it is clear that he believed that primary drives are 'subject to historical modification', he also created in *Eros and Civilization* the overwhelming impression that men and women are characterised by their possession across the centuries of a common instinctual structure regardless of specific historical circumstances; and he was at pains to take Freud's part against the neo-freudian attempt to historicise this basic structure. Marcuse's 1930s general and flexible definition of human essence as being the sum of past achievements and future possibilities was thus replaced in *Eros and Civilization* with a more specific and limited definition in terms of freudian man.

Let us conclude Marcuse's account of the domination-liberation-domination dynamic: in terms of the struggle between Eros and Thanatos this process results in the weakening of the former at the expense of the latter and this is potentially disastrous, for aggression can build up to such a degree that civilisation may destroy itself — a possibility that haunts both Freud's *Civilization and its Discontents* and Marcuse's *Eros and Civilization*.

Yet for all this *Eros and Civilization* was an intensely optimistic work, in that it maintained that contemporary civilisation can blossom and achieve a thoroughly liberated existence under the rule of a new reality principle and in this respect raised that central question of Marcuse's social theory: 'What is authentic existence, and how is it at all possible?' Marcuse's grounds for optimism were two-fold. Firstly he used Freud against Freud by pointing to 'the tabooed insights of psychoanalysis' which exploded Freud's own gloomy prognostications, and secondly, he pointed to societal tendencies which invalidated Freud's own social assumptions.

With regard to the first of these grounds his discussion focused on the nature of the life instinct (Eros). As Lipshires pointed out, Freud used the word 'Eros' in two different ways: firstly as conterminous with sexuality; and, secondly and much more broadly, as the opponent of the death instinct whose function in Freud's words 'is to establish ever greater unities and to preserve them thus — in short, to bind together'.[35] Marcuse appropriated this distinction but, with greater clarity, termed the first usage 'sexuality' and only the second one 'Eros' whilst acknowledging that it was also legitimate to term sexuality 'Eros'. Thus at one point in *Eros and Civilization*, for example, he suggested that 'it may not be accidental that Freud does not rigidly distinguish between Eros and sexuality',[36] and in other places he distinguished Eros from 'mere sexuality';[37] in short, he considered sexuality to be a not fully developed form of Eros which was nonetheless capable of being transformed into the latter. The life instinct is the ultimate source of civilisation, as Marcuse stated in a 1955 lecture: 'Civilization arises from pleasure: we must hold fast to this thesis, in all its provocativeness'.[38] Thus he used one of Freud's own conceptions

52

as the starting point for an attack on Freud's conservatism, since it was Freud's contention that civilisation could only exist on the basis of extensive erotic repression. Having established that Marcuse believed that the roots of civilisation are erotic, let us now consider Marcuse's account of how these erotic roots constantly reassert themselves even in the repressed environment of the performance principle — a process he termed 'the return of the repressed'.

Marcuse's most interesting remarks on this issue were centred around his discussion of the 'perversions'. In his opinion the 'perversions' have upheld sexuality as an end in itself against the surplus repression demanded by the appropriate reality principle. In the case of contemporary society, for example, they in effect champion the 'pleasure principle' against the 'performance principle':

> Against a society which employs sexuality as a means for a useful end, the perversions uphold sexuality as an end in itself; they thus place themselves outside the domination of the performance principle and challenge its very foundation.[39]

In particular, the 'perversions' involve 'polymorphous perverse' sexuality, which is sexuality not limited by space and time either with regard to its subject or its object, and as a result, they threaten to re-sexualise the organism; consequently, the 'perversions' serve as a knife at the throat of the performance principle which, for the perpetuation of its existence, requires a thoroughly desexualised individual. Marcuse referred to the senses of taste and of smell, whose erotic use would allow people to relate to one another in a way totally incompatible with the current exploitative organisation of labour:

> Smell and taste give, as it were, unsublimated pleasure per se ... They relate ... individuals immediately ... Such immediacy is incompatible with the effectiveness of organized domination, with a society which tends to isolate people, to put distance between them and to prevent spontaneous relations and the 'natural' animal-like expressions of such

relations.[40]

Narcissism and homosexuality are similarly cited as 'perversions' which contain this revolutionary potential; and ancient mythology is used to elucidate this point. Narcissus, in the Greek myth, fell in love with his own image without knowing that the image was in fact his own: for Marcuse, Narcissus therefore represented the triumph of disinterested contemplation of beauty. Using the freudian notion of primary narcissism, Marcuse related this myth to psychoanalysis, pointing to the infant's lack of any conception of discrete entities apart from itself, where it experiences the universe as pure, undifferentiated extension. Such primary narcissism therefore contains an effective libidinisation of the body and the environment and, consequently, an indictment of the desexualisation to which the performance principle gives rise:

> Narcissism may contain the germ of a different reality principle: the libidinal cathexis of the ego (one's own body) may become the source and reservoir for a new libidinal cathexis of the objective word — transforming the world into a new mode of being.[41]

Given that Marcuse saw contemporary sexuality as being dangerously restricted, it is not surprising that he saw in homosexuality a protest against this restriction. In fact he went even further and accorded this critical status to paedophilia — which at the present time is probably the most tabooed of all sexual modes; he used the folk-hero Orpheus as a symbol, for Orpheus spurned the love of women and instead (in the words of Ovid) gave 'his love to tender boys ... enjoying the springtime and first flower of their growth'. In doing so Orpheus was protesting against the restriction of Eros entailed in procreative sexuality. Orpheus, according to Marcuse:

> rejects the normal Eros, not for an ascetic ideal, but for a fuller Eros. Like Narcissus, he protests against the repressive order of procreative sexuality.[42]

In his courageous examination of the progressive component of the 'perversions' Marcuse cut a lonely figure in the marxist tradition. In the case of paedophilia Marx and Engels simply reflected the dominant climate of opinion of their time and saw such activities as inherently degrading. Thus Engels in *The Origin of the Family, Private Property and the State* added to his analysis of the role of the ancient Athenian family in the oppression of women:

> But the degradation of the women recoiled on the men themselves and degraded them too until they sank into the perversion of boy-love, degrading both themselves and their gods by the myth of Ganymede.[43]

At this time, the most widely-held 'progressive' view on homosexuality could be seen in the nationalistic socialist Ferdinand Lasalle, who combined distaste with a call for toleration and when a colleague, J.B. von Schweitzer, was tried and convicted for a homosexual offence, said:

> What Schweitzer did isn't pretty, but I hardly look upon it as a crime ... In the long run, sexual activity is a matter of taste and ought to be left up to each person, so long as he doesn't encroach upon someone else's interests. Though I wouldn't give my daughter in marriage to such a man.[44]

As Jeffrey Weeks has rightly pointed out, the liberal toleration argument has by and large represented the 'progressive' limit of the left. Thus Bernstein and Bebel called at the turn of the century for the abolition of the homophobic paragraph 175 of the Imperial German Penal Code, but in the context of a firm belief in the normality of heterosexuality and of a total lack of understanding of the revolutionary nature of sexuality itself.[45] In the socialist tradition, Marcuse's only real predecessor in this respect was a man of whom he never himself appeared to be aware — Edward Carpenter. Carpenter, although he espoused a now discredited theory that homosexuality — or as he termed it, Uranism — represented a third sex, nonetheless argued like Marcuse that the homosexual impulse both challenged the current repressive mode of sexuality and anticipated the life to come:

> Sex still goes first, and hands, eyes, mouth, brain follow: from the midst of belly and thighs, radiate the knowledge of self, religion and immortality,[46]

and:

> It is possible that the Uranian spirit may lead to something like a general enthusiasm of humanity, and that the Uranian people may be destined to form the advance guard of that great movement which will one day transform the common life by substituting the bond of personal affection and compassion for the monetary, legal and other external ties which now control and confine society.[47]

According to Marcuse, not all 'perversions' possess a progressive function and he made a distinction between practices which are incompatible with repressive civilisation and those which are incompatible with civilisation itself. Sadism as practised in a free libidinal relationship is entirely different from that practised coercively, for example by the SS in concentration camps. The latter is a form of what he came to term 'repressive desublimation', a temporary explosion of frustrated sexuality which manifests all the marks of its suppressed history and which the system can allow to occur, for it in no way threatens its repressive organisation. On the contrary, it reinforces the system, for such a process:

> manifests itself in the hideous forms so well known in the history of civilization; in the sadistic and masochistic orgies of desperate masses, of 'society élites', of starved bands of mercenaries, of prison and concentration camp guards. Such a release of sexuality provides a periodically necessary outlet for unbearable frustration; it strengthens rather than weakens the roots of instinctual constraint; consequently it has been used time and again as a prop for suppressive regimes.[48]

Neither was Marcuse advocating the 'perversions' as an end in themselves. To abandon exclusive heterosexuality in favour of exclusive homosexuality would be to miss the point, which is to libidinise the organism and its environment by transforming sexuality into Eros, in which the erotic impulse would not be partial (i.e. centred exclusively on objects such as the genitals, members of the opposite sex, etc.) but all-encompassing: the body in its entirety; all individuals; the whole environment. Such a transformation must be a total and collective affair if the polymorphous perverse nature of sexuality is to unite and not to isolate. For this reason, Marcuse maintained that the 'perversions' in a repressive society have a tendency to develop into isolating neuroses. Similarly, Reich was criticised for believing that a mere release of sexuality, bigger and better orgasms, is equivalent to a progress in freedom.

Mere sexuality is therefore to be transformed into Eros. In the life to come Eros is to involve the 'self-sublimation of sexuality' or 'non-repressive sublimation'.[49] As ever, the concept of labour was never very far from Marcuse's thinking and in *Eros and Civilization* it was central to his discussion of what exactly 'non-repressive sublimation' entails.

Two developments occurred in Marcuse's concept of labour between his writings of the 1930s and *Eros and Civilization*. Firstly the notion of total automation entered his distinction between labour in the realm of necessity and in the realm of freedom. Whilst he still adhered to Marx's distinction in *Capital III*, he came to regard total automation as a means whereby humanity can reduce necessary labour to an absolute minimum:

> The elimination of human potentialities from the world of (alienated) labor creates the preconditions for the elimination of labor from the world of human potentialities.[50]

In the years which followed, Marcuse was to constantly cite what, in a non-pejorative sense, he termed a 'utopian' element in Marx's thinking enshrined in one particular passage of the *Grundrisse*. The references to this passage, which occurs in

Notebook VII, the chapter on Capital, are so numerous in his works after *Eros and Civilization* that it is worth quoting from it at length:

> But to the degree that large industry develops, the creation of real wealth comes to depend less on labour time and on the amount of labour employed than on the power of the agencies set in motion during labour time, whose 'powerful effectiveness' is itself in turn out of all proportion to the direct labour time spent on their production, but depends rather on the general state of science and on the progress of technology, or the application of this science to production ... Labour no longer appears so much to be included within the production process; rather, the human being comes to relate more as a watchman and regulator ... He steps to the side of the production process, instead of being its chief actor. In this transformation, it is neither the direct human labour he himself performs nor the time during which he works, but rather the appropriation of his own general productive powers, his understanding of nature and his mastery over it by virtue of his presence as a social body — it is, in a word, the development of the social individual which appears as the great foundation-stone of production and of wealth.[51]

The second development in Marcuse's concept of labour was the notion of labour as play. He derived this notion from outside the marxist tradition, for its roots are in the work of Schiller and Fourier (as we have seen, the concept of play had been an early interest of his). From Schiller's *On the Aesthetic Education of Man*, Marcuse derived the notion of a 'play impulse' which he implicitly equated with free objectification or labour in the realm of freedom:

> it is the play of life, beyond want and external compulsion — the manifestation of an existence without fear and anxiety, and thus the manifestation of freedom itself.[52]

Reality ceases to be the basis of human slavery and instead

becomes the ground for human fulfilment. From Fourier he derived the notion of '*travail attrayant*', labour that was inherently pleasurable because it was based on an '*attraction passionnée*' in the nature of humanity, which enabled it at the same time to satisfy its passions and to build civilisation.[53] Once Marcuse had added to these notions the freudian hypothesis of the civilisation-building capacity of the libido, he could confidently assert that 'the liberation of Eros could create new and durable work relations'.[54]

The second ground for optimism in *Eros and Civilization* lay in the social developments which suggested that the basis for repression was gradually becoming eroded. These developments were two-fold; firstly, Marcuse believed that the decline of the family was weakening the link between individuals and the performance principle and secondly, that increasing automation was undermining the rationale for surplus instinctual repression. With regard to the first of these — the decline of the family — Marcuse cited in *Eros and Civilization* the Institute's 1936 study on Authority and the Family *Studien über Autorität und Familie* to which he himself had contributed. Horkheimer had argued in this work that, in the period of bourgeois liberalism, the family had been the crucial agent of socialisation, ultimately because the pater-familias was then the source of economic well-being for all his dependents. In the era of monopoly capitalism the father ceased to be the sole bread-winner, and thus his authority passed on to extra-familial institutions thereby weakening the socialising role of the family.[55] In *Eros and Civilization* Marcuse used this analysis to argue that with the decline of family socialisation the performance principle is gradually deprived of its traditional instinctual grounding:

> The living links between the individual and his culture are loosened ... the repressive force of the reality principle seems no longer renewed and rejuvenated by the repressed individuals. The less they function as the agents and victims of their own life, the less is the reality principle strengthened through 'creative' identifications and

sublimations.[56]

The second development pointed in the same direction. Increasing automation effectively prevents the individual from gaining any element of realisation from his or her work, which simultaneously renders the worker's labour largely superfluous and destroys any remaining identification the worker may have with his or her work:

> The human energies which sustained the performance principle are becoming increasingly dispensable. The automization of necessity and waste, of labor and entertainment, precludes the realization of individual potentialities in this realm ... The ideology of scarcity, of the productivity of toil, domination, and renunciation is dislodged from its instinctual as well as rational ground.[57]

As Marcuse was to state explicitly in later works, Marx (in the *Grundrisse*) had anticipated that the growth of automation would sound the death-knell of the capitalist mode of production, since its basis — the exploitation of labour — could be undermined. Marx's argument followed on directly from the passage which we quoted earlier:

> The theft of alien labour time, on which the present wealth is based, appears as a miserable foundation in the face of this new one, created by large-scale industry itself. As soon as labour in the direct form has ceased to be the wellspring of wealth, labour time ceases and must cease to be its measure, and hence exchange value [must cease to be the measure] of use value. The surplus value of the mass has ceased to be the condition for the development of general wealth, just as the non-labour of the few, for the development of the general powers of the human head. With that, production based on exchange value breaks down ...[58]

What then of the proletariat? What indeed, for it makes no appearance whatever in *Eros and Civilization*. This can partly be explained by the implicitly rather than explicitly marxist perspective of the work; Marx is not cited once, and Freud is consequently presented as a far more radical thinker than is actually the case. Such reticence cannot be taken as a sign that Marcuse was abandoning a marxist perspective — for in his other writings of this period the validity of marxism was clearly asserted. It is worth quoting a passage from his 1958 preface to Raya Dunayevskaya's *Marxism and Freedom* to illustrate the continuity between Marcuse's social theory of the 1930s and that of the 1950s: the same old ideas are there — interpretation of the past; political activity; current tendencies; the ideal of the life to come; the dubious value of predictions; the unfalsifiability of the theory; and the subjection of Marx and Engels to a historical materialist analysis:

> Inasmuch as Marx's and Engels's notion of the development of mature capitalism and of the transition to socialism was elaborated prior to the stage at which its 'verification' was envisaged, marxian theory may be said to imply predictions. But the essential character of this theory denies such designation. Marxian theory is an interpretation of history and defines, on the basis of this interpretation, the political action which, using the given historical possibilities, can establish a society without exploitation, misery and injustice. Thus, in its conceptual structure as well as in its political practice, marxian theory must 'respond' to the historical reality in process: modification of the theoretical concepts and of the political practice to be guided by them is part of the theory itself.[59]

However, whilst the marxist perspective was retained the same cannot be said of the theory of proletarian revolution which Marcuse considered to be in need of revision for two main reasons — firstly, to take into consideration the decline of revolutionary consciousness in the working class, and secondly to take account of the developing anomymity of the class enemy. In respect of the first of these reasons, Marcuse pointed to the dominance of reformist and conformist attitudes amongst the working class, a process so pervasive that it could not be explained by having recourse to notions of the aristocracy of labour. The proletariat as a class in advanced capitalist society had ceased to be an oppositional force:

> Under the leadership of their ... bureaucracy the situation of a major part of [the proletariat] changed from one of 'absolute negation' to one of affirmation of the established system.[60]

We shall leave a fuller analysis of Marcuse's position as regards the role of the proletariat until the next chapter; it will suffice here to say that underlying *Eros and Civilization* was a belief that the proletariat could not be expected to fulfil the revolutionary role outlined for it by Marx.

A second complicating factor was that of the increasing difficulties involved in identifying the class enemy which, whilst it had not disappeared, was nonetheless becoming concealed behind the spurious rationality of the modern administered society:

> With the rationalization of the productive apparatus, with the multiplication of functions, all domination assumes the form of administration. At its peak, the concentration of economic power seems to turn into anonymity.[61]

Thus even where anger and frustration remain, the proletariat seems to lack a legitimate object against which to direct these emotions, for the top-hatted and paunchy capitalist, insofar as such a being ever existed, has been replaced by the apparently blameless functionaries of the caring society: 'Smiling colleagues, busy competitors, obedient officials, helpful social workers who are all doing their duty and who are all innocent victims.'[62]

Eros and Civilization was thus the first of Marcuse's major works to detach itself from the notion of proletarian revolution. Class revolution gave way to human liberation, a transition most clearly revealed in his concept of the 'Great

Refusal',[63] a term derived from a rather unlikely source — *Whitehead's Science and the Modern World*. The Great Refusal consists of all those ideas and actions which reject the current reality principle in favour of a qualitatively superior life, and Marcuse singled out for special discussion its manifestations in the realms of art, philosophy and sexuality. This concept was clearly operative in his work of the 1930s, though during this earlier period he made some attempt to place it in an overarching theory of class revolution; no such attempt is even contemplated in *Eros and Civilization*.

4. Technological Rationality

Marcuse anticipated the deeply pessimistic thesis of his *One-Dimensional Man* over twenty years earlier, in a 1941 article 'Some Social Implications of Modern Technology', which dealt with the growth of what he termed 'technological rationality'. In this article, he made an initial distinction between technological rationality and individualistic rationality: individualistic rationality characterised the free economic subject of early capitalism and was essentially critical in that it:

> derived freedom of action from the unrestricted liberty of thought and conscience and measured all social standards and relations by the individual's rational self-interest'.[1]

With the development of capitalism, the economic basis supporting individualistic rationality was undermined as the demands of the market induced greater and greater mechanisation and rationalisation; thus early mercantile and industrial capitalism became transformed into monopoly capitalism and in the course of this transformation, individualistic rationality was transformed into technological rationality. Whereas individual rationality is critical and oppositional, technological rationality is essentially conformist in that it 'establishes standards of judgement and fosters attitudes which make men ready to accept and even to introject the dictates of the apparatus'.[2]

In developing this argument Marcuse, again anticipating *One-Dimensional Man* in this respect, was quite responsive to the work of bourgeois sociology. He cited Thorstein Veblen's *The Instinct of Workmanship* to show how mechanisation reduces the worker to a mere appendage of the machine, for in the workplace activity is reduced to 'a sequence of semi-spontaneous reactions to prescribed mechanical norms',[3] individual spontaneity is replaced by conformity to a mechanical process which legitimates itself in terms of efficiency. Weber's concept of rationalisation is used to help explain how 'the mechanics of conformity' spreads into the social sphere in general — how in Weber's terms formal rationality becomes dominant. The element of this process with which Marcuse was principally concerned was the gradual disappearance of critical thought and action in the face of systematic rationalisation. Under capitalism, technological rationality has wrongfully become cloaked with the mantle of reason itself, and this is the result of two main developments: at the individual level, an introjection of systemic values; and at the collective level, the incorporation and effective neutralisation of the organised opposition.

At the individual level the 'expediency, convenience and efficiency' of the life created by modern industry appear to render any objection to it irrational and, consequently, these achievements seem to belie the possibility of any credible alternative; this in turn results in external control in the service of domination being converted into 'rational' self-control. In this way the inadequate present is frozen and its liberating possibilities remain unactualised: the individual under capitalism 'is losing his ability to abstract from the special form in which rationalization is carried through and is losing his faith in its unfulfilled potentialities'.[4] This is complemented by the absorption of oppositional movements into the system, a process which is all the more insidious in that these movements retain the title of opposition but not its function. Trade unions and left-wing political parties, for example, although they retain the support of the grass roots, in fact only pursue the true interests of that support at the rhetorical level. Thus in the case of the socialist opposition in Europe in general:

> the critical rationality of its aim was subordinated to the technological rationality of its organization and thereby

'purged' of the elements which transcended the established pattern of thought and action.[5]

A poisonous dynamic is operating in such groups, which develop into bureaucratic mass organisations.

The term 'mass' was used pejoratively by Marcuse in this 1941 article to refer to a bogus collectivity which cannot be qualitatively but only quantitatively distinguished from 'the individual', for as a member of the masses the individual remains unchanged in essence. Any unity in the masses is fundamentally spurious, as it is the unity of 'the atomic subjects of self-preservation who are detached from everything that transcends their selfish interests and impulses'.[6] Thoroughly imbued with technological rationality, any aspirations towards change on the part of the masses refer only to changes within the framework of the given: 'The coordinated masses do not crave a new order but a larger share in the prevailing one'.[7]

The growth of the masses is accompanied by a growth of bureaucracy. Once more the influence of Weber is apparent — a fact which Marcuse admitted when he cited Weber's remark that bureaucracy is 'the universal concomitant of modern mass democracy',[8] though of course he did not accept the conservative implications drawn by Weber from his theory of bureaucracy. Marcuse was particularly concerned with the development of 'a hierarchical organization of private bureaucracies' for, in their claim of overcoming the atomisation created by standardisation through specialisation, the highly irrational interests they represent are concealed behind the banner of reason; thus they foster 'a delusive harmony between the special and the common interest'.[9]

In a society imbued with technological rationality the truths of critical rationality lose their subversive potential and become part of the established culture, their effectiveness being inversely proportional to their 'popularity'. Thus the critique of political economy becomes a weapon used, for example, by competing business groups or by governments for anti-monopoly purposes: 'it is propagated by the columnists of the big press syndicates and finds its way even into the popular magazines and the addresses to manufacturers associations';[10] all of which testifies to the utter impotence of the critique. The 1941 article painted a depressing picture of the individual in advanced capitalism which anticipated 'one-dimensional man', an individual unable to transcend the given either cognitively or in practice; thus over two decades before the later work, Marcuse was writing:

> Today the prevailing type of individual is no longer capable of seizing the fateful moment which constitutes his freedom. He has changed his function; from a unit of resistance and autonomy, he has passed to one of ductility and adjustment.[11]

On resuming his writing career in the 1950s, following periods of study at the Soviet studies centres at Columbia and Harvard, Marcuse sought to extend the application of the concept of technological rationality to an analysis of the USSR. In *Soviet Marxism* (published in 1958) he pointed to a number of features — common to both advanced capitalism and the Soviet system — which included the replacement of individual autonomy by centralised regimentation, the organisation and rationalisation of competition, the joint rule of economic and political bureaucracies, and the co-ordination of the masses through communications, entertainment, industry and education. He took pains to point out the fundamental difference between the systems, their distinct dominant ideologies (which in the case of the Soviet Union could not be crudely characterised as a simple rationalisation of partial interests), the different property relationships (nationalised as opposed to private), and the differing prospects for fundamental change; however insofar as the Soviet Union had sought as an absolute priority to catch up with the West industrially, it too had succumbed to the spread of technological rationality.

For Marcuse, mechanisation and rationalisation could have two essentially antagonistic outcomes: firstly, the tendency outlined in *Eros and Civilization*, where technological progress and the development of large industry was seen as the means whereby individuals could be freed from the unfulfilling labour of the realm of necessity, and would thus become able to develop fully their faculties in the realm of freedom; secondly, however, these developments could also generate 'attitudes of standardized conformity and precise submission to the machine'.[12] In *Soviet Marxism* it was the latter development which he considered to have characterised the genesis of the Soviet system, and the phenomenon of Stakhanovism, for example, was viewed as symptomatic of the triumph of technological rationality — a triumph greatly facilitated by nationalisation and centralisation:

> If nationalization and centralization of the industrial apparatus goes hand in hand ... with the subjugation and enforcement of labour, as a full-time occupation, progress in industrialization is tantamount to progress in domination: attendance to the machine, the scientific work process, becomes totalitarian, affecting all spheres of life.[13]

According to Marcuse, Soviet society is dominated by a bureaucracy whose economic base lies in the control rather than the ownership of the means of production, and since this bureaucratic control in no way represents (or is accountable to) the 'official' owners of the means of production, namely the people, Marcuse was willing to call the bureaucracy a class. He was clearly unhappy with this definition, and tended to use the term caste or class with inverted commas; furthermore, though he was willing to describe the Soviet system as a class society, he was not willing to describe it as a capitalist or state capitalist society, seeing it rather as a new type of social formation which could not be adequately described in terms of the capitalism-socialism spectrum.

He rejected analyses which overstress the role of a dictator in Soviet development, for even Stalin could not override the imperatives of the system as a whole; nor can power be seen to lie with a specific group within the bureaucracy for the bureaucracy is composed of a large number of conflicting interests — agricultural, industrial, military, and so on. The bureaucracy as a whole is itself constrained by two factors; firstly the Central Plan which, although it is the product of the bureaucracy, is also the result of complex horse-trading amongst the various interests, interests which are not arbitrary but which reflect the basic trends in Soviet society, such as concentrating on heavy industry as a means of catching up with the West; secondly, the bureaucracy is subject to 'competitive terror', the systemic ubiquity of which prevents any one individual or group feeling either totally immune from it or totally in control of it. Marcuse's conclusion was clear:

> The Soviet bureaucracy ... does not seem to possess a basis for the effective perpetuation of special interests against the overriding general requirements of the social system on which it lives.[14]

We shall leave until later Marcuse's analysis of the prospects for qualitative change in the Soviet Union and first examine his conception of the role the Soviet system plays in stabilising advanced capitalism; his conception of this role can be termed his 'enemy from without' thesis, and it comprises an ideological and an economic dimension. With regard to the first dimension, the Soviet system fulfils a potent ideological function in advanced capitalism as the outsider which legitimates imperialist co-ordination at all levels — the wicked communism against which the West can be presented as the guarantor of supposed common interests. This ideological function bears further fruit in that it legitimates the development of a 'defence economy' which enables capitalism to freeze its inherent contradictions by sustaining technological and economic growth. The net effect of 'the enemy without' has been to promote, since the end of the second world war, an organised capitalism very different from the mode of production with which Marx was familiar:

> the conflicting competitive interests among the Western nations were gradually integrated and superseded by the

fundamental East-West conflict, and an inter-continental political economy took shape ... susceptible to a planned regulation of that blind 'anarchy' in which Marxism saw the root of capitalist contradictions.[15]

This stabilisation and hierarchical integration of the capitalist world has laid the foundations for what had been the bad dreams of Hilferding's *Finanzkapital* and Kautsky's *Der Imperialismus*:

> For Marxism the capitalist world had never come closer to the dreaded spectre of a 'general cartel' which would replace the anarchy of capitalist production and distribution by ultraimperialist planning.[16]

This inevitably leads us on to Marcuse's 1964 work *One-Dimensional Man*, which integrated, developed and in some respects modified his earlier analyses of advanced industrial societies, and which particularly concentrated on the nature and function of technology in these societies. In his 1941 article, to which I have already referred, Marcuse distinguished 'technics' from 'technology', defining the former as 'the technical apparatus of industry, transportation, communication' and the latter as the social use of that apparatus; whereas technics is politically neutral, technology contains a political a priori, a position reiterated in *Soviet Marxism*:

> Modern machinery is susceptible to capitalist as well as socialist utilization. This amounts to saying that mature capitalism and socialism have the same technical base, and that the historical decision as to how this base is used is a political decision.[17]

In this work, Marx is cited as an authority for this position; his remark in *The Poverty of Philosophy* that the 'hand-mill gives you society with the feudal lord; the steam-mill, society with the industrial capitalist'[18] is interpreted as not exhausting the possible relationships between instruments and modes of production for, as he argued elsewhere, it is the social mode of production and not technics which in marxism is the primary analytic category in the examination of social formations.[19]

In *One-Dimensional Man* the distinction between a political technology and a neutral technics was collapsed; Marcuse now considered that both contain a political a priori in that productive instruments are inherently purposeful quite apart from any purpose intended in their social use: 'the technological society is a system of domination which operates already in the concept and construction of techniques'.[20] This is reflected at the terminological level, where Marcuse often used 'technology' as a synonym for 'technics' as, for example, in a 1964 piece on Max Weber:

> Not only the application of technology but technology itself is domination ... Specific purposes and interests of domination are not foisted upon technology 'subsequently' and from the outside; they enter the very construction of the technical apparatus.[21]

A number of influences can be detected in Marcuse's expanded concept of technology. Horkheimer and Adorno's work, particularly their joint *Dialectic of Enlightenment* published in 1947 is one such influence: its central thesis is that the thought and behaviour of bourgeois society (which they termed 'enlightenment') has replaced an earlier inter-penetrative relationship between humanity and nature with one based upon humanity's repressive mastery of nature. 'Enlightenment behaves towards things as a dictator toward men. He knows them in so far as he can manipulate them.'[22] Science and technology represent both humanity's power over nature and its alienation from it — an alienation which in turn characterises the relationship between individuals. This thesis is clearly echoed in *One-Dimensional Man*:

> As a technological universe, advanced industrial society is a political universe, the latest stage in the realization of a specific historical project — namely, the experience, transformation, and organization of nature as the mere

stuff of domination.[23]

A freudian infusion can also be detected, and it is centred on the psychic roots of technology. Technological progress is fed, according to Freud, by the diversion of primary destructiveness away from the ego to the eternal world. As he put it in *Civilization and Its Discontents*:

> The instinct of destruction, moderated and tamed, and, as it were, inhibited in its aim, must, when it is directed towards objects, provide the ego with the satisfaction of its vital needs and with control over nature.[24]

It was Marcuse's contention in *Eros and Civilization* that the destructive instinct was less sublimated than the libido in advanced industrial society and although the former could be harnessed to the service of Eros to provide the material base of civilisation, this necessarily involved the 'violation' of nature:

> extroverted destruction remains destruction: its objects are in most cases actually and violently assailed, deprived of their form, and reconstructed only after partial destruction; units are forcibly divided, and the component parts forcibly rearranged. Nature is literally 'violated'.[25]

This reveals the thoroughly sinister element in technology, for the destructive instinct as a derivative of the death instinct ultimately resists serving Eros and aims at the destruction of life itself:

> through constructive technological destruction, through the constructive violation of nature, the instincts would still operate toward the annihilation of life.[26]

The constructive role of technology is thus a by-product of an essentially deadly process.

Finally, we might mention the influence of Marcuse's former teacher Heidegger, to whose work on technology he referred in *One-Dimensional Man*. Heidegger, following Husserl, attacked the cartesian dualism of consciousness and the world, and its concomitant notion of nature as an object to be calculated and ultimately manipulated by the human subject. Thus technology, as it is thoroughly imbued with this repressive dualism, is by no means a neutral phenomenon and it cannot be analysed in technical terms alone. For Heidegger, modern technology was essentially manipulative:

> The revealing that rules in modern technology is a challenging, which puts to nature the unreasonable demand that it supply energy which can be extracted and stored as such.[27]

Marcuse, in *One-Dimensional Man*, appreciatively paraphrased Heidegger on the social nature of technology:

> The science of nature develops under the technological a priori which projects nature as potential instrumentality, stuff of control and organization. And the apprehension of nature as (hypothetical) instrumentality precedes the development of all particular technical organization ...[28]

The opening sentence of the first chapter of *One-Dimensional Man* encapsulates the central contention of the work: 'A comfortable, smooth, reasonable, democratic unfreedom prevails in advanced industrial civilization, a token of technical progress.'[29] Through the organisation of their technological base, Marcuse argued, contemporary industrial societies have generated ubiquitous, non-transcendent needs and suffocated transcendent needs; they are consequently to be considered 'totalitarian' regardless of the degree of institutional pluralism they possess. The mechanisms involved in this triumph of technological rationality emerged in Marcuse's analysis of two mainstays of the Great Refusal — art, and sexuality.

In his 1941 article 'Some Social Implications of Modern Technology', Marcuse noted that the destruction of individuality by large-scale industry was extending to the art-forms of individualism as the rarefied high culture of classical capitalism was replaced by the mass culture of organised capitalism. At the time, Marcuse considered that this process contained the seeds of progress, for since the culture of classical capitalism derived its truth from its representation of 'the potentialities of man and nature which were excluded or distorted in reality'[30] its debunking indicated the extent to which individual creativeness and originality had been rendered unnecessary and the degree to which the foundations had been laid for the positive supersession of this culture and its classic consumers and producers. He expressed the optimistic opinion that in the face of fascist barbarism the 'ideal' contained in liberalist culture had 'become so concrete and so universal that it grips the life of every human being' and that 'Under the terror that now threatens the world ... everyone knows what freedom means, and everyone is aware of the irrationality in the prevailing rationality.'[31]

Such optimism is absent from the 1958 *Soviet Marxism*, in which the sad fate of art in the Soviet Union is seen as both a product of special Soviet factors and as exemplifying a general trend in advanced industrial societies and one he now considered thoroughly baleful — the neutralisation of art as a source of critical consciousness. The peculiarly Soviet aspect of this process is said to stem from the demand of the Soviet ruling stratum for a realist art appropriate to socialism; yet since only the hypostatised general interest is in fact 'represented' in that society, this stratum is forced to suppress the artistic expression of interests which are unfulfilled and to enforce a thoroughly conformist art. If the Soviet Union was in fact what it claimed to be, argued Marcuse, then given the premise of the link between social progress and the obsolescence of art, it would not require art at all; but since it is not what it claims, necessary art is attacked and unnecessary art is promoted. Soviet aesthetics, Marcuse remarked acidly, 'insists on art, while outlawing the transcendence of art. It wants art that is not art, and it gets what it asks for.'[32]

He saw the Soviet attack on surrealism and atonality as evidence of a phenomenon common to all advanced industrial societies, namely the retreat of critical consciousness from traditional realist and tonal modes, as the latter are rendered harmless by a process of chronic trivialisation which blunts transcendent cognition by crass over-familiarity. In a desperate bid to remain authentic, art has to revolt against conventional style, form and substance:

> the more reality controls all language and all communication, the more irrealistic and surrealistic will art tend to be, the more will it be driven from the concrete to the abstract, from harmony to dissonance, from content to form.[33]

In *One-Dimensional Man*, the prospects for the survival of even these 'extreme' modes are not considered good as two-dimensional culture, with its critical dimension of reality, is seen to be systematically and seemingly inexorably reduced to one dimension. In his work, which is primarily concerned with advanced industrial capitalist societies (principally the USA), the mass reproduction and consumption of art-forms is contrasted with traditional elitist culture, in which ritualisation of art facilitated a distancing process:

> The salon, the concert, opera, theatre are designed to create and invoke another dimension of reality. Their attendance requires festive-like preparation; they cut off and transcend everyday experience.[34]

One-dimensional society has largely eliminated this ritualisation. By selling the 'Greats' on budget LPs and in paperbacks, by making culture available to all, the critical function of the artistic oeuvres so marketed is lost. Bach has become background music to the washing-up, and Dickens the Book at Bedtime. As Marcuse wrote in a 1965 article, culture has become popular at the expense of its critical role:

> the integration of cultural values into the established society cancels the alienation of culture from civilization ... The result: the autonomous, critical contents of culture become educational, elevating, relaxing — a vehicle of adjustment.[35]

Like the tamed classics, the oeuvres of modern mass

culture are castigated in *One-Dimensional Man*, which is irredeemably hostile to most modern artistic production. Thus, for example, the representation of sexuality in the artistic landmarks of the classical and romantic periods — which is said to be 'absolute, uncompromising, unconditional' — is contrasted with the 'wild and obscene, virile and tasty, quite immoral' (and quite uncritical) treatment in the work of such varied modern luminaries as Eugene O'Neill, Tennessee Williams, Vladimir Nabokov and William Faulkner.[36] Similarly the traditional literary heroes — 'the artist, the prostitute, the adultress, the great criminal and outcast, the warrior, the rebel-poet, the devil, the fool', whose artistic representation indicted and refuted the reality which produced them, are contrasted with their modern counterparts — 'The vamp, the national hero, the beatnik, the neurotic housewife, the gangster, the star, the charismatic tycoon', who serve to affirm rather than to negate their society.[37] Marcuse, in *One-Dimensional Man*, clearly underestimated the critical dimension in much modern artistic production as he engaged in the dangerous procedure of not merely asserting the possibility of an authentic art but of attempting to specify its content. From Engels's claim that the 'complete inability to tell a story and create a situation ... is characteristic of the poetry of true socialism',[38] through Lukács's 'Narration establishes proportions, description merely levels',[39] to Zhdanov's accusation that Prokofiev, Shostakovich and others were guilty in their music of 'formalist distortions and anti-democratic tendencies',[40] the marxist tradition is littered with highly dubious attempts to do just this.

Marcuse also, in his analysis of the neutralisation of the classics, was guilty of exaggerating the extent to which repressive contexts obliterate critical contents and this was partly due to a misuse of the concept of repressive desublimation. Art, which for Marcuse necessarily involved the sublimation of Eros had, he maintained, undergone repressive desublimation in one-dimensional society as the mediated gratification characteristic of two-dimensional culture was replaced by an immediate gratification compatible with the existing reality. This insight was not applied sparingly enough by Marcuse, and he consequently underestimated the power of works of art not simply despite but even because of their mass diffusion. This exaggerated use of the concept of repressive desublimation is particularly noticeable in his analysis of sexuality in *One-Dimensional Man*.

Karl Miller characterised Marcuse's stance on the principal role of sexuality in one-dimensional society as 'An orgy a day keeps the revolution away'[41] and, albeit flippantly, thereby captured its broad sense which is that a liberalisation of sexual mores has effectively managed the conflict between the pleasure principle (the demands of Eros) and the reality principle by allowing a controlled gratification which does not threaten the surplus instinctual repression still required by the performance principle:

> The range of socially permissible and desirable satisfaction is greatly enlarged, but through this satisfaction, the pleasure principle is reduced — deprived of the claims which are irreconcilable with the established society. Pleasure, thus adjusted, generates submission.[42]

Such repressive desublimation is made possible by a number of factors; Marcuse mentioned the reduction of dirty and heavy physical labour, the availabilty of cheap attractive clothing, beauty culture and physical hygiene, the needs of the vast advertising industry, the destruction of privacy in modern architecture, and the de-eroticisation of the environment through mechanisation, which repels libidinal cathexis and encourages intensified, localised sexuality.

As in the case of art, Marcuse was being over-pessimistic. His own earlier work suggested that the nature of sexuality was such that (granted a number of important reservations) its release tended to be thoroughly beneficial; in addition the sexual renaissance of youth in particular during the years which followed the publication of *One-Dimensional Man* suggested that the liberalisation of sexuality, so vilified in that work, was the first stirring of and a major contributing factor to the 'erotic revolution' which Marcuse himself was to welcome so enthusiastically in the late 1960s and which, although it was eventually contained, helped to bear lasting fruit, for example in the form of the contemporary feminist and gay movements.

Common to Marcuse's strictures on art and sexuality in his 1964 work was the notion of the demise of the autonomous subject, which rendered obsolete the freudian concept of man — a notion succinctly anticipated in Adorno's 1944 aphorism: 'In many people it is already an impertinence to say "I".'[43] Marcuse considered the term 'introjection' to be an inappropriate description of the process whereby individuals reproduce and perpetuate external social controls, for it implied the existence of an inner dimension (conscious and unconscious) which was distinct from external reality; it was precisely this dimension which, Marcuse believed, mass production and distribution had effectively eradicated. The relationship between individuals and between them and their society is now an immediate, mechanical identification so thorough that autonomy is considered a curse:

> The antenna on every house, the transistor on every beach, the jukebox in every bar or restaurant are as many cries of desperation — not to be left alone, by himself, not to be separated from the Big Ones, not to be condemned to the emptiness or the hatred or the dreams of oneself.[44]

It is not surprising in the light of the above that in *One-Dimensional Man* the prospects for human liberation are not considered to be rosy; on the other hand, they are not considered totally hopeless, as the introduction to that work makes clear:

> *One-Dimensional Man* will vacillate throughout between two contradictory hypotheses: (1) that advanced industrial society is capable of containing qualitative change for the foreseeable future; (2) that forces and tendencies exist which may break this containment and explode the society.[45]

Neither will it come as any surprise that the proletariat as the revolutionary class does not figure prominently in the 1964 work except in a critical light. We are fortunate in possessing in *Soviet Marxism* Marcuse's analysis of the vicissitudes of the proletariat in marxist theory, an examination of which may serve as a prelude to our analysis of his treatment of this class in *One-Dimensional Man*.

In *Soviet Marxism*, he cited a number of Engels's remarks concerning the latter's experience of the English proletariat to show that the co-founder of critical theory was aware of the possibility of the embourgeoisement — Marcuse used the term *Verbürgerlichung* — of the proletariat due to the ability of capitalism not simply to sustain itself but actually to increase the standard of living of the majority of its population.[46] Engels's letter of October 1858 to Marx was cited as an example:

> the English proletariat is actually becoming more and more bourgeois, so that this most bourgeois of all nations is apparently aiming ultimately at the possession of a bourgeois aristocracy and a bourgeois proletariat alongside the bourgeoisie.[47]

He also pointed to the difference between the pure model of capitalism presented in *Capital I* and the subsequent volumes, in which the historical reality of capitalism is the object of study and in which the counter-trends capitalism develops against its inherent contradictions are discussed. Despite this it was Marcuse's contention that Marx and Engels conceived of the socialist revolution exclusively in terms of proletarian revolution:

> The revolution was to be the direct organized action of the proletariat as a class — or it was not at all. Marx and Engels did not recognise any other agent of the revolution nor any 'substitute' for it ...[48]

Marcuse considered that Lenin's interpretation of the growth of reformism in the proletariat in terms of the development of a 'labour aristocracy' had grossly underestimated the structural changes that capitalism had undergone, including fundamental changes in the position of the proletariat (changes which Lenin's revolutionary strategy implicitly acknowledged). In this respect the revisionists had a clearer grasp of the development of capitalism than did the radicals:

> Even prior to the First World War it became clear that the 'collaborationist' part of the proletariat was quantitatively and qualitatively different from a small upper stratum that had been corrupted by monopoly capital, and that the Social Democratic Party and trade union bureaucracy were more than 'traitors' — rather that their policy reflected pretty exactly the economic and social condition of the majority of the organised working classes in the advanced industrial countries.[49]

Orthodox marxist explanations of this phenomenon in terms of a temporary 'immunisation' facilitated by the growth of labour productivity, labour militancy and monopolistic surplus profits failed to grasp that the unthinkable international capitalist consolidation was in the process of developing.

In *One-Dimensional Man* Marcuse analysed in greater depth the transformation of the proletariat which, he maintained, was occurring in advanced capitalist societies. The first important factor he highlighted was the reduction of 'the quantity and intensity of physical energy expended in labour'[50] as a result of mechanisation. He maintained that the classical notion of the proletariat necessarily included the sheer physical misery and pain involved in labour, factors which helped to make the proletariat the 'living denial' of its society and which helped to implant in it the overwhelming need to overcome this state of affairs. In advanced industrial capitalism, however, increasing mechanisation reduces the need for such physical anguish and, in consequence, reduces the proletariat's own perception of its still inhuman position in capitalism: the ever-more-complete mechanisation of labour in advanced capitalism, while sustaining exploitation, modifies the attitude and the status of the exploited.[51]

A second factor is job assimilation in advanced capitalism, where the white-collar sector grows at the expense of the blue-collar. Mechanisation is converting the labourers into supervisors, directors, thereby integrating them into the ranks of white-collar supervisors with all the consequences of the first factor and the additional loss of the traditional class prerogative of the proletariat to halt production by withdrawing its professional skills — 'the power to stop a process which threatened him with annihilation as a human being'.[52]

The third factor is one which we have already encountered in *Eros and Civilization*, namely the effects of the transfiguration of domination into administration, where the capitalists and their managers appear to be mere functionaries in a broader system, which deprives the proletariat of a legitimate target for any residual hatred and frustration.[53] At the point of production this process reinforces, and is in turn reinforced by, the equalisation of life styles made possible by advanced industrial capitalism which (within the context of continued — if veiled — exploitation) legitimates the illusion of the classless good life and testifies to the 'downward' diffusion of false needs:

> If the worker and his boss enjoy the same television programme and visit the same resort places, if the typist is as attractively made-up as the daughter of her employer, if the Negro owns a Cadillac, if they all read the same newspaper, then this assimilation indicates not the disappearance of classes, but the extent to which the needs and satisfactions that serve the preservation of the Establishment are shared by the underlying population.[54]

The conclusion Marcuse drew from this is that since social change requires a 'vital need for it',[55] when the proletariat becomes thoroughly supportive of the established way of life — even if it were to gain control of the productive process — this would not result in qualitative change but would merely 'prolong the [established way of life] in a different setting'.[56]

Before moving on to examine Marcuse's remarks on the

positive prospects for qualitative change in advanced capitalism, let us first turn to his assessment in *One-Dimensional Man* of the prospects for such change in the third world and in the Soviet Union.

One-Dimensional Man concerned itself with those third world countries which were in the early stages of industrialisation and which retained strong pre-technological cultures, notably Egypt and India. The crucial factor in the current development of these societies was said to be the two super-powers, whose existence tended to generate two distorted paths of development: either neo-colonialism based on the third world's dependence on super-power capital for primary accumulation, or rapid and potentially brutal industrialisation as these societies sought to remain independent of Moscow or Washington. In this international context Marcuse thought it unlikely that a third path based on indigenous tradition and resources would be successful — even if the considerable internal barriers to such development were overcome.[57] With regard to the Soviet Union, the fact that the mode of production was not the separation of the immediate producers from the means of production, as was necessarily the case in capitalism, meant for Marcuse that it was possible to remove the Soviet ruling stratum 'without exploding the basic institutions of society'.[58] The nationalised productive process allowed qualitative change to be conceived of in political rather than in economic terms (which would ultimately involve the withering away of the state, party and plan). He was aware that it was not in the interests of the bureaucracy for such a political revolution to occur but he optimistically speculated that 'the need for the all-out utilization of technical progress'[59] in the context of co-existence with capitalism might ultimately reveal the irrationality of bureaucratic domination and so undermine the position of that stratum. *One-Dimensional Man* presented no evidence to suggest that Marcuse considered such a development to be imminent.

Marcuse's stipulation that qualitative change presupposed a vital need for it meant that in advanced capitalism the 'absolute negation' of that mode of production had to be sought either beyond or beneath the great conformist consensus, and in the closing paragraphs of *One-Dimensional Man* he briefly alluded to an assortment of marginal groups which he maintained were clearly beneath this consensus:

> underneath the conservative popular base is the substratum of the outcasts and the outsiders, the exploited and persecuted of other races and other colours, the unemployed and the unemployable.[60]

They are considered to be the living negation of a society into which they are not integrated and probably never will be. However he admitted in a lecture of the same period[61] that these groups lacked the necessary consciousness and organisation to be immediate subjects of the transition to socialism Rather, they are to be considered as part of the Great Refusal, materially needy agents who might just conceivably join up with those beyond the conservative consensus and cement an alliance of 'the most advanced consciousness of humanity, and its most exploited force'.[62] He accepted that this possibility was no more than a chance and the very brevity of his remarks on this topic is a token of the despondency that pervades *One-Dimensional Man*. In the light of this, it would be wrong to see in the last pages of that work anything more than the most fleeting anticipation of the more precise and fuller formulations he developed in his later work in response to the social and political developments of the ensuing years.

5. Liberation

Before the optimistic *An Essay on Liberation* of 1968, there came a transition period in Marcuse's work, in which the pessimism characteristic of *One-Dimensional Man* gradually lessened. In this period Marcuse sought possible avenues of escape from what he considered to be the vicious circle which characterised revolutionary prospects in advanced industrial society:

> for new, revolutionary needs to develop, the mechanisms that reproduce the old needs must be abolished. In order for the mechanisms to be abolished, there must first be a need to abolish them.[1]

His 1965 essay 'Repressive Tolerance' can be considered the first important product of this period for, basing itself on the thesis of one-dimensionality, it examined strategies and tactics of transformation through an analysis of the concept of toleration. A noticeable oddity of this work is that it appears to have been addressed to two distinct subjects — radical minorities and popular radical governments — and, in a rather confusing fashion, it moved between these two, although it is clear from both the text and from Marcuse's retrospective comments that the governmental subject was used as a heuristic device in what was really an address to an actual subject — the minorities of the Great Refusal.

The conclusion of the work was provocatively stated in its opening paragraph:

> the realization of the objective of tolerance would call for intolerance toward prevailing policies, attitudes, opinions,

and the extension of tolerance to policies, attitudes, and opinions which are outlawed or suppressed.[2]

Whilst accepting that tolerance is an end in itself, Marcuse added the crucial rider that this only applies when social conditions allow genuine, universal toleration to prevail; until then toleration is, to a greater or lesser extent, necessarily subordinated to over-riding conservative or radical principles. He divided the 'repressive toleration' underlying the proclaimed general toleration of advanced capitalism into two aspects — passive and abstract. Passive toleration involves mechanical, non-reflective acceptance of that which on reflection is unacceptable and differs fundamentally from the active critical tolerance which had been so effective at the beginning of the bourgeois epoch. With respect to the arms race, police action against 'subversives', neo-colonial massacres, and so forth, he maintained that:

> the people ... are educated to sustain such practices ... Tolerance is extended to policies, conditions, and modes of behaviour which should not be tolerated because they are impeding, if not destroying, the chances of creating an existence without fear and misery.[3]

Passive toleration is complemented at the institutional level by abstract toleration whose official, formal neutrality to both Right and Left sustains the status quo because of the induced predisposition of individuals in one-dimensional society to believe the former rather than the latter; for example in the publication of a positive and a negative article on the country's intelligence agencies, the positive will be believed at the expense of the negative because of the pre-formed image of these agencies in the people's mind:

> official tolerance granted to the Right as well as to the Left, to movements of aggression as well as to movements of peace, to the party of hate as well as to that of humanity ... refrains from taking sides — but in doing so it actually protects the already established machinery of

discrimination.[4]

The struggle for universal tolerance requires the reactivation of critical tolerance together with its necessary element of intolerance. At the level of specifics — who is to do what, when, how, and to whom — 'Repressive Tolerance', although more positive and optimistic than *One-Dimensional Man*, was on the whole vague and imprecise even in comparison with the 1964 work and certainly in comparison with the work which was to flow from Marcuse's pen in the succeeding years. In its perception of the necessity and possibility of radicalising the educational sphere, however, the work anticipated a major (some might say obsessive) focus of attention of this later writing.

In this period, two developments in particular alerted Marcuse to the radicalisation of sections of the student body in the USA. The first of these was the movement of students from northern universities (which had begun in the early sixties and which included some of Marcuse's own students) down south to help blacks gain basic civil rights. He responded angrily, in a 1965 reply, to Marshall Berman's jibe in a review of *One-Dimensional Man* that this work had not taken the work of the civil rights workers into account; Marcuse claimed that on the contrary, the work was written for precisely such people who were 'risking their lives in the south', 'because of their flat refusal to stand any longer for systematic injustice'.[5] This experience of brute oppression, he later maintained, so traumatised the students concerned that it led to their radicalisation:

> they saw for the first time how this free democratic system really looks, what the sheriffs really are up to, how murders and lynchings of blacks go unpunished though the criminals are well known.[6]

This was complemented by the second development, the role of students in the opposition to the war in Vietnam — which in his opinion opened the eyes of many of them to the nature of their society.

By 1967 Marcuse's perception of student activism had developed into a fairly detailed and positive theory, the essence of which was stated in a lecture he gave that year at the Free University of Berlin:

> You know that I hold today's student opposition to be a decisive factor of transformation: surely not, as ... an immediate revolutionary force, but as one of the strongest factors, one that can perhaps become a revolutionary force.[7]

In his work of this year (which included *An Essay on Liberation*, the bulk of which was written prior to the events of May 1968), Marcuse highlighted a number of areas in which radical student activity suggested that new needs were emerging. With respect to educational establishments for example, insofar as these had become props of the established order by carrying out harmful research for governments and corporations and by maintaining a bogus neutrality on social and political issues, student agitation was helping to bring about changes for the better; and where this failed, alternatives were being set up in which critical thought could flourish.[8] Secondly there was what he termed the 'moral-sexual' rebellion of the students (and of other sections of the 'youth movement'), which involved the rediscovery within themselves of the instinctual basis of freedom, the development of that vital desideratum of qualitative change — needs that are the 'absolute negation' of the current order. Drug-taking, although an artificial, temporary and potentially escapist process does nonetheless enable people 'to see, hear, feel new things in a new way'[9] through the dissolution of the ego of one-dimensional society. In the linguistic sphere the young rebels subvert one-dimensional language by splitting the totalitarian unity of object, term and meaning. For example, the aura of legitimate authority suggested by the term 'police' is shattered by substituting the term 'pig'; so too the replacement of the repressive clinical-legal term 'homosexual' with the more positive implications of the term 'gay'. When sexual obscenities are used the desublimation of culture is facilitated; by calling policemen 'motherfuckers' (or as Marcuse somewhat fastidiously put it: addressing them as 'men who have perpetuated the unspeakable Oedipal crime'),[10] the radicals are demystifying the actual, instinctual dynamics of law and order, for the violence of the police is a product of the guilt they feel about the betrayal of the life instincts which is involved in the order they protect: 'They slept with the mother without having slain the father, a deed less reprehensible but more contemptible than that of Oedipus.'[11] A third and final area he noted was the 'drop out' phenomenon (which included many former students), in which the consumer society and its repressive needs are rejected and withdrawn from:

> What we have here is ... the simple refusal to take part in the blessings of the 'affluent society'. That is in itself one of the qualitative changes of need. The need for better television sets, better automobiles, or comfort of any sort has been cast off. What we see is rather the negation of this need. 'We don't want to have anything to do with all this crap.'[12]

Marcuse maintained that if it remained isolated from the majority and its concerns, the student opposition would merely be the nucleus of a revolution that would never occur, and he repeatedly denied paternity of the notion that the student activists were a revolutionary force in themselves, or that the hippies were the heirs of the proletariat. Their role was as a 'catalyst', communicating rediscovered needs to broader sections of the population — including the proletariat, without whom qualitative change was impossible. His perception of the problem associated with such a strategy was apparent in his admission of July 1967 that: 'We are no mass movement. I do not believe that in the near future we will see such a mass movement.'[13]

In *One-Dimensional Man* Marcuse had speculated on the possible unification of those beyond one-dimensional society and those beneath it; and in the following years his refined analyses of the privileged were paralleled by those of the under-privileged — in particular of the black population of the United States who, like the youthful opposition, Marcuse took to be the absolute negation of their society but from a basis of poverty and brutal, overt oppression — not pampered affluence. In a number of respects Marcuse considered this section of society to be a potentially revolutionary force. Their appalling living conditions — packed tightly together in major urban centres — facilitated both organisation and effective action against economically and politically important targets, and in this respect recalled the geographical disadvantages and advantages of the classical European proletariat.[14] At the same time a thorough-going linguistic rebellion was said to be occurring in black culture, paralleling that of the young militants, as the most venerated and sublimated concepts of white culture were desublimated and redefined: a case in point being the metamorphosis of the concept 'Soul'. Black music was also portrayed as a further mode of desublimation, which bypassed the highly sublimated and affirmative oeuvres of the western tradition and liberated the 'mindless' joy of Eros:

> The black music, invading the white culture, is the terrifying realization of 'O Freunde, nicht diese Töne!' — the refusal now hits the chorus which sings the Ode to Joy, the song which is invalidated in the culture that sings it ... In the subversive, dissonant crying and shouting rhythm, born in the 'dark continent' and in the 'deep South' of slavery and deprivation, the oppressed revoke the Ninth Symphony and give art a desublimated, sensuous form of frightening immediacy, moving, electrifying the body, and the soul materialized in the body.[15]

Counter-tendencies did however exist and in Marcuse's opinion, threatened the effectiveness of black rebellion. The low level of political awareness tended to be centred on racial rather than class issues. Also, the existence of a black bourgeoisie served as a source of division, and the marginal status of the majority of blacks in the production process made their occupational power of obstruction slight and rendered them particularly expendable if their radicalism became manifest.[16] Finally, radical black art, like much explicit art in general, tended to lack what Brecht termed an estrangement effect (Verfremdungseffekt) — the sense of dissociation from the given necessary for cognitive transcendence, without which art becomes a mere source of temporary release, easily handled by the market of one-dimensional society.[17]

Whilst the ghetto population formed part of the internal underprivileged of US capitalism, the external counterpart was constituted by the masses of the third world. By 1967 the gloomy perspective of *One-Dimensional Man* on third world development had to some extent diminished in the face of the prospering Cuban revolution, the cultural revolution in China, the Vietnamese struggle for national liberation and the disintegration of the unity of the international communist order. Marcuse argued that one effect of the spectre of liberation raised by these events was the reinforcement of the convergence tendency of the two advanced industrial systems, resulting in:

> some sort of common interest between the Soviet Union on the one side and the United States on the other.
>
> In a sense, this is indeed the community of interests of the 'haves' against the 'have nots', of the Old against the New.[18]

Although the conditions of existence of the 'have-not' people make them the absolute negation in and for themselves of capitalism, Marcuse was adamant that their struggles by themselves would only debilitate that system materially and ideologically and not destroy it, for its destruction was the *prerequisite* for the ultimate success of these struggles. Twenty years earlier in *Soviet Marxism*, he had spelled out that, for Marx, socialist revolution was to be the result of exploding contradictions in a fully-matured capitalist system; and had claimed this to be Lenin's opinion also: 'and not even the triumph of the Bolshevik Revolution made ... Lenin ... abandon this conviction'.[19] In *An Essay on Liberation* he said quite plainly: 'The chain of oppression must break at its strongest link.'[20] What is required is the 'confluence of forces of change in the centres of advanced capitalism with those in the third world'.[21]

It should be noted in passing that the vagueness of the term 'confluence' is symptomatic of Marcuse's failure to consider in any depth what (apart from the shaky ground of a shared opposition to aspects of capitalist society) could possibly unite the disparate elements of the Great Refusal in political activity and a concomitant failure to specify — other than at the highest level of abstraction — precisely how these forces were to be co-ordinated both prior to and during a revolutionary upsurge. With regard to the latter point, whatever mileage he could extract from the supplementary argument that the specificity of revolutions precluded detailed anticipation was to be exhausted by the events of May 1968, which compelled him to concretise his analyses. Before turning to this, however, we shall briefly examine what was to prove to be the final development in Marcuse's long-standing preoccupation with the relationship between the realm of freedom and the realm of necessity.

In his 1967 lecture 'The End of Utopia', Marcuse further developed the work-as-play thesis of *Eros and Civilization* by effectively collapsing the distinction between the realm of freedom and the realm of necessity or — at the very least — by drawing its 'anti-utopian' sting. The origin of the distinction in Marx's work was seen as an indication of the latter's inability to fully anticipate the eventual obsolescence of the current forces of production and of their attendant limitation of human possibility, most notably the immutable element of unfulfilment in labour for necessities (though as Marcuse had previously argued and was to reiterate in other works of this period, the *Grundrisse* contained a more utopian conception). Freedom and necessary labour could no longer be conceived of as mutually exclusive and the qualitative leap involved in the transition to a free society would be most clearly expressed by 'letting the realm of freedom appear within the realm of necessity — in labor and not only beyond labor'.[22]

The climax of the developing optimism that characterised Marcuse's work between his 66th and his 70th year came with what in fact turned out for him to be the very mixed blessing of the events of May-June 1968 in Paris. Whilst the influence of Marcuse on these events has on the whole been overestimated there can be no doubt as to their effect on him. The unbelievable had happened — a mass protest against the given:

> for one reason or another the time had come when hundreds of thousands, and, as we see now, millions of people didn't want it any more. They didn't want to get up in the morning and go to their job and go through the same routine and listen to the same orders and comply with the same working conditions and perform the same performances. They simply had enough of it.[23]

Marcuse was particularly excited by what he maintained had been the catalytic role of the students *vis-à-vis* the working class. His belief in the success of the campaign of sending students into the factories to talk to the workers was most graphically illustrated in the account he gave of the first major street battle between students and police:

> Their young leader, Daniel Cohn-Bendit, who organised the barricades and was with them all the time till six in the morning, when the street battle was lost, said 'Now there is only one thing to be done: the General Strike'. The following Monday the strike order was followed 100%.[24]

He spelled out the lesson to be learnt:

> it should once and for all heal whoever suffers from the inferiority complex of the intellectual. There isn't the slightest doubt that, in this case, the students showed the workers what could be done and that the workers followed the slogan and the example set by the students. The students were literally the avant-garde ...[25]

This working-class receptivity, explained in terms of the class's relative poverty and its militant tradition, went against the grain of the thesis of *One-Dimensional Man*, in which it had been argued that, despite their traditions, the working classes of the less developed capitalist countries such as France and Italy were going down the same path of integration as their US counterparts. Given his previous analyses, Marcuse's excitement at the fact that the revolutionary wave last seen in Europe in the early twenties was once more on the move must, to say the least, have concealed an element of surprise.

A further source of surprise was provided by the pockets of radicalism in the technical intelligentsia — Serge Mallet's 'new working class'. Back in 1941, in an attack on Burnham's 'managerial revolution' thesis, Marcuse had distinguished between managers functionally determined by the material process of production (engineers, technicians, production managers, plant superintendents) and those whose function was determined by the requirements of profitability (executives, corporation managers) and had argued that although the former were immediate producers, their privileged position in the division of labour aligned them with capital rather than labour.[26] This was still his position in 1967 when pressed to comment on Mallet's thesis: 'My objection to Mallet's evaluation of technicians is that precisely this group is among the highest paid and rewarded beneficiaries of the system'.[27]

He further argued, in the light of his *One-Dimensional Man* strictures on technology, that the technical intelligentsia invariably conceived of revolution as technocratic revolution — which was essentially the mere streamlining of oppression. In *An Essay on Liberation* where the latter argument was repeated and salvation seen in terms of the productive process being determined by groups 'with needs and goals very different from those of the technocrats', the surprise of the May-June events intruded in the form of a footnote: 'The existence of such groups among the highly qualified technical personnel was demonstrated during the May-June rebellion in France'.[28] Once more the unexpected had happened.

In the case of the festive rebellion of the students and their allies, Marcuse threw caution to the wind. Here was the new sensibility in action tranforming the one-dimensional society into a qualitatively different form; Eros itself roamed the streets of Paris free from its traditional constraints:

A utopian conception? It has been the great, real, transcending force, the 'idée neuve', in the first powerful rebellion against the whole of the existing society, the rebellion for the total transvaluation of values, for qualitatively different ways of life: the May rebellion in France. The graffiti of the 'jeunesse en colère' joined Karl Marx and André Breton: the slogan 'l'imagination au pouvoir' went well with 'les comités (soviets) partout'; the piano with the jazz player stood well between the barricades; the red flag well fitted the statue of the author of *Les Misérables*; ... The new sensibility has become a political force.[29]

The profound effect on Marcuse of these events and of the renaissance of 'new left' activity in general is conveyed in a moving speech he made in December 1968:

We cannot wait and we shall not wait. I certainly cannot wait. And not only because of my age. I don't think we have to wait. And even I, I don't have any choice. Because I literally couldn't stand it any longer if nothing would change. Even I am suffocating.[30]

As the tide of the student movement in Europe and America began to ebb, such extravagant hope faded and Marcuse set to work analysing the nature and causes of this development — an exercise which yielded three main conclusions. Firstly that the tendencies outlined in *One-Dimensional Man* had proved to be far stronger than the counter-tendencies of the later works. When asked in a 1973 interview if the events of Paris 1968 had shown the book on one-dimensionality to be over-pessimistic, Marcuse answered: 'It seems to me that unfortunately what I said in my book has been corroborated.

Unfortunately!'[31] His own fame seemed to him to reinforce this melancholic conclusion: as a pet bogey-man, a part of the intellectual scenery of pluralist society, he could say what he liked — one-dimensional society was quite capable of processing it. When asked in late 1969 how he analysed the 'Marcuse phenomenon', he replied:

> I think that my own self-analysis is a simple one. By which I mean that there is nothing in heaven or on earth which publicity is unable to integrate into the established system.[32]

However, and this was his second conclusion, the most advanced one-dimensional society (the USA) was, given a different national and international context, weaker than in the early sixties and was being forced to go on to the offensive, supplementing its covert mechanisms of repression with overt ones. In response to major foreign policy setbacks, an ailing economy and domestic protest, the state with the support of the conservative majority was violently purging opposition, and fascism — the final resort of terrified capitalism — could not be ruled out as a possible development.[33] Finally, Marcuse concluded that the protest movement needed to rethink its strategies and tactics both to meet the new counter-offensive and to overcome inherent weaknesses of previous praxis, which in the main involved a move beyond 'the heroic period of beautiful spontaneity, of personal anti-authoritarianism, of hippy rock and shock'[34] to more prosaic, thoughtful and organised activity.

Marcuse's long-term hopes for the future of the most advanced one-dimensional societies rested upon a belief that capitalism would tend to produce its own determinate negation through a broadening of the base of exploitation and the fostering of transcendent needs — developments which, he maintained, were anticipated in Marx's own work. With respect to the first of these the normal economic processes of monopoly capitalism, combined with ever-increasing 'state management', were resulting in a growth of both the tertiary sector and the technical intelligentsia involved in material production; which meant that:

> ever more strata of the formerly independent middle classes become the direct servants of capital, occupied in the creation and realization of surplus value while being separated from control of the means of production.[35]

Thus *Gesamtkapital* (the requirements of capital as a whole) results in the development of a *Gesamtarbeiter* (collective labour force), a process which, as Marcuse illustrated, was outlined in an earlier version of a sixth chapter of *Capital*, in which Marx wrote:

> No longer the individual laborer but rather the socially combined labor power becomes the actual agent of the collective work process. The various competing labor powers which constitute the productive machine as a whole participate in very different ways in the immediate production of commodities (here rather products). One individual works with his hands, another with his head, one as a manager, engineer, technologist, et cetera, the other as overseer, a third as direct manual laborer or mere helper. Thus more and more functions of labor power are being subsumed under the immediate concept of productive labor and the workers under the concept of productive workers. They are directly exploited by capital ... [The combined activity of the collective laborer results] immediately in a collective product which is at the same time a sum-total of commodities, and it is a matter of indifference whether the function of the individual worker, who is only a member of this collective laborer, is more remote or close to manual labor ... The activity of this combined labor power is its immediate productive consumption by capital — self-realization of capital, immediate creation of surplus value.[36]

Marcuse made no attempt to minimise the obstacles to this process, particularly the hierarchy of privilege within the collective labour force, nor did he suggest (in keeping with a fundamental belief) that such a process, either alone or in conjunction with others, will inevitably result in a transition to a free society. What the process will do, according to Marcuse, is to provide a potential social grounding for the second long-term development he highlighted: the emergence of transcendent needs.

Capitalism, said Marcuse, is gradually falling victim to its own success. Whereas previously the rising standard of living necessitated the creation of needs that could be satisfied by the market, 'it is now fostering transcending needs which cannot be satisfied without abolishing the capitalist mode of production'.[37] He cited the following passage in the *Grundrisse* as evidence of Marx's anticipation of this process:

> The great historic quality of capital is to create ... surplus labour, superfluous labour from the standpoint of mere use value, mere subsistence; and its historic destiny is fulfilled as soon as, on one side, there has been such a development of needs that surplus labour above and beyond necessity has itself become a general need arising out of individual needs themselves — and, on the other side, when the severe discipline of capital, acting on succeeding generations, has developed general industriousness as the general property of the new species.[38]

Marcuse saw this process operating at two levels: in the sophisticated demands of the critical elites (the call for ecological, sexual change, etc.)[39] and in the 'spontaneous' attitudes and activity of the conservative majority (wildcat strikes, cynicism over the work ethic: 'Inner worldly asceticism goes badly with the consumer society'[40] etc.); however, both reflect a belief that a better life is possible.

In Marcuse's conception, a crucial component of the better life and the one we have not really examined so far, is a transformed relationship between humanity and nature. It was in *Eros and Civilization* that he had first speculated about the possibility of a non-repressive relationship between humanity and nature and had traced this perennial idea through the philosophical, aesthetic, mythological, psychological and anthropological traditions (in the case of the latter he had pointed to Margaret Mead's revelation that the Arapesh see nature not as an object to be dominated but as 'a "garden" which can grow while making human beings grow'[41]). *One-Dimensional Man* distinguished between a repressive and a liberating mastery of nature, in which the latter would involve the 'pacification of existence' through the use of a technology so transformed that it would signal the end of technology as it is currently conceived:

> 'Pacified existence'. The phrase conveys poorly enough the intent to sum up, in one guiding idea, the tabooed and ridiculated [sic] *end* of technology, the repressive final cause behind the scientific enterprise. If this final cause were to materialize and become effective, the Logos of technics would open a universe of qualitatively different relations between man and man and man and nature.[42]

Marcuse's latest and most comprehensive treatment of this notion is to be found in his early seventies piece 'Nature and Revolution'. Marx's analysis of the relationship between the human species and nature as presented in his early work is contrasted favourably with his later development in the marxist tradition (and by implication in Marx's own mature work), where the species is conceived of as being necessarily involved in a zero-sum game with nature in which its growth is dependent on the subjugation of nature — which is thus a false universalisation of the experience of individuals under capitalism. By contrast the *Economic and Philosophical Manuscripts* speak of a human appropriation of nature through which, in Marcuse's words, nature 'becomes the congenial medium for human gratification to the degree to which nature's own gratifying forces and qualities are recovered and released';[43] in short, nature is seen as a subject-object. However, Marcuse considered that even this formulation was inadequate, for it still did not fully recognise nature as a subject in its own right:

Marx's notion of a human appropriation of nature retains something of the hubris of domination. 'Appropriation', no matter how human, remains an appropriation of a (living) object by a subject. It offends that which is essentially other than the appropriating subject and which exists precisely as object in its own right — that is as subject![44]

The non-exploitative negation of appropriation involves 'surrender, "letting be", acceptance ...'[45] Yet Marcuse pulled back from absolute idealism; in a phrase recalling his early concept of labour as burden, he concluded: 'nature is not a manifestation of "spirit", but rather its essential limit' — humanity and nature can never be completely reconciled.[46]

A sense of the limitation of radical activity, revealed in this quotation, is most noticeable in the output of Marcuse's final years and is especially apparent in his treatment of aesthetics. Of particular note is his rejection of the 'end of art', a notion he had flirted with in earlier writings. According to Marcuse, since art remains committed to the Idea (Schopenhauer), to the universal, and since the tension between the Idea and reality, between the universal and the particular cannot be overcome except in absolute idealism, art would remain a desideratum in any society, socialist included:

> The institutions of a socialist society, even in their most democratic form, could never resolve all the conflicts between the universal and the particular, between human beings and nature, between individual and individual. Socialism does not and cannot liberate Eros from Thanatos.[47]

At best, art in such a society would lose its elitist character but could never legitimately lose its estrangement from reality. The 'end of art' could only occur when people could no longer distinguish 'between true and false, good and evil, beautiful and ugly, present and future'[48] — a development indicative not of socialism but of 'perfect barbarism', though as Marcuse added darkly: 'such a state is indeed a historical possibility'.[49]

Conclusion

Marcuse died on 29 July 1979, ten days after his 81st birthday. An attempt to form an overview of his long theoretical career is immediately confronted by the encyclopaedic range of his work, the product of a personal amalgam of eclecticism and criticism which refused to be bound by the conventional division of intellectual labour or to succumb to the puritan insularity characteristic of all that is most arid in the marxist tradition.

It is in the area of fundamental theoretical influences that the eclectic nature of Marcuse's social theory is most apparent; the influence of such figures as Heidegger and Hegel, Horkheimer, Adorno and Freud was, as I have argued, of crucial importance to the genesis of his work, a fact attested to by the various labels applied to him over the years: freudo-marxist, hegelian-marxist, heidegger-marxist, to name but a few. This eclecticism is also obvious in the colourful procession of marginal groups that winds its way through his work: the sexual outlaws, inhabitants of the ghettos, hippies and the outsiders of all kinds who make up the social base of that peculiarly marcusian concept — the Great Refusal. The critical impulse in Marcuse also casts its net wide and takes seriously the monumental task which the negative moment of the dialectical world view entails. As I have attempted to show, his works over the years present an exhausting, if not exhaustive, series of critiques of a multitude of objects: philosophical traditions, psychological theories, modes of development, social and political systems and so on, in response to the obligation to criticise the whole.

Marcuse wielded the weapon of criticism with particular

ruthlessness against a number of the sacred cows of marxism — for example the classical concept of the proletariat, where he believed that an uncritical stance *vis-à-vis* the concept of the founders of the tradition had resulted in a widespread bogus universalisation or fetishisation of the historically limited. He maintained that a process of constant conceptual refinement involving the discarding of any concepts that failed to adequately interpret current reality and its genesis or to express the possibilities inherent in the present was fundamental to a sound marxist analysis; and I have sought to show how his commitment to this principle was demonstrated in the marked theoretical variations displayed in his works of differing periods.

This concern with the critical, the negative, did not occur in isolation in Marcuse's work but rather as part of a dialectical analysis whose function was to reveal the grounds for overcoming negativity. He had an unshakeable belief that some light could be found in the gloomiest state of affairs and in all of his major works, even in the bleak *One-Dimensional Man*, an attempt was made to highlight transcendent tendencies.

This in turn leads us on to what I have argued is the fundamental question which permeates Marcuse's work: 'What is authentic existence, and how is it at all possible?'. Although he maintained that the existence proper to a free society could not be anticipated in all its rich detail before its establishment, he nonetheless felt that it was necessary and legitimate both to define the essence of such an existence and to point to anticipations of it. Writing for most of his life in and for societies which were experiencing a steady increase in living standards, he believed that it was vital to distinguish between authentic existence and the satisfied enslavement of consumer society; thus in 1967, when students pressed him on the effectiveness of 'humanitarian' arguments against the Vietnam War, he in effect argued that the appeal to the human essence contained in such arguments was the only effective basis for a critique of societies of plenty:

If I really radically exclude humanitarian arguments, on what basis can I work against the system of advanced capitalism? If you only operate within the framework of technological rationality and from the start exclude historically transcendent concepts, that is negations of the system — for this system is not humane, and humanitarian ideas belong to the negation of the system — then you continually find yourself in the situation of being asked, and not being able to answer, the question, What is really so terrible about this sytem, which continually expands social wealth so that strata of the population that previously lived in the greatest poverty and misery today have automobiles, television sets, and one-family houses? What is so bad about this system that we dare take the tremendous risk of preaching its overthrow?[1]

In his depiction of the life to come, Marcuse over the years displayed great boldness and breadth of vision, searching through the storehouse of human experience for concepts and images which conveyed the essence of this existence — a process which involved a continuous tension between his 'utopian' aspirations and his equally strong sense of the immutable limits of human happiness. Throughout the various forms it adopted in his work, this vision of the future had as its core a conception of the individual as a free creative subject who is able and willing to develop fully all the facets of existence repelled by the current reality:

When the associated individuals themselves have taken over the direction of the life process and have made the totality of social relations the work of their reason and freedom, what man is in himself will be related to his existence in a new way. The formerly contingent and 'inessential' will now represent the fulfilment of the most authentic potentialities. Man will then have to be 'defined' not as a free rational being in opposition to contingent conditions of life but as the free and rational creator of his conditions of life, as the creator of a better and happier life.[2]

In this book, I have pointed to two broad areas in Marcuse's work where useful criticism could be developed. The first refers back to his eclectic impulse and prompts the question: to what extent are the theoretical sources appropriated by Marcuse from outside the marxist tradition actually compatible with that tradition? I have pointed to instances where Marcuse's attempt to give his social theory a non-marxist theoretical infusion has resulted both in a distorted interpretation of this external source, through a suggestion that it is more radical than is the case, and in the introduction of concepts which seem ill at ease amongst mainstream marxist concepts. This is most apparent in his appropriation of Freud, where he not only made highly dubious claims concerning the critical aspects of that thinker's work but somewhat uncritically imported certain of the latter's equally dubious concepts (the model of human instincts and the notion of transhistorical psychic determinism) into his social theory.

Secondly, there is the question of whether Marcuse's use of the concepts of 'absolute negation' and of the 'Great Refusal' both reflected and further contributed to an excessive concentration on marginal rebelliousness and an inadequate concentration on the complex dynamics of advanced capitalism in general, and on the nature of what he termed the 'conservative majority' in particular. If this is the case, then this would certainly help to explain, for example, the puzzling shifts of interpretation displayed in his works of the sixties and seventies where the social system which seemed virtually invincible in *One-Dimensional Man* was on its way to collapse in *An Essay on Liberation* (a bare four years later), only to reappear relatively secure in as little time again.

I do not wish , however, to end this book on a critical note. The weaknesses in Marcuse's work should in no way diminish its importance and continuing relevance for those who are seriously committed to a creative and dynamic marxism. His neglect by the left does not testify to theoretical sophistication on its part but, on the contrary, indicates a fundamental theoretical inadequacy which should be both deplored and, more importantly, overcome.

References

Introduction

1. M. Jay, 'The Metapolitics of Utopianism', *Dissent*, XVII, 4, 1970, p. 342.
2. P. Breines (ed.), *Critical Interruptions*, New York: Herder and Herder 1970, p. IX.
3. P. Walton and A. Gamble, *From Alienation to Surplus Value*, London: Sheed and Ward 1976, p. 103.
4. T. Roszak, *The Making of a Counter Culture*, London: Faber and Faber 1971, p. 101.

1. Authenticity and Labour

1. Biographical material in S. Lipshires, *Herbert Marcuse: From Marx to Freud and Beyond*, Cambridge (Mass): Schenkman Publishing Co. 1974; M. Jay, *The Dialectical Imagination*, London: Heinemann Educational Books 1973.
2. S. Kean and J. Raser, 'A Conversation with Herbert Marcuse', *Psychology Today*, February 1971, p. 35.
3. H. Marcuse, *Schiller-Bibliographie unter Benutzung der Trämelschen Schiller-Bibliothek*, Berlin: S. Martin Fraenkel 1925.
4. The pre-Frankfurt School work of Marcuse has been opened up to the English-speaking world by the journal *Telos*. In addition to its translations of a number of important early articles by Marcuse, *Telos* has provided useful introductions to these, namely P. Piccone and A. Delfini, 'Herbert Marcuse's Heideggerian Marxism', *Telos* 6, 1970, D. Kellner, 'Introduction to "On the Philosophical Foundation of the Concept of Labor" ', *Telos* 16, 1973, M. Schoolman, 'Introduction to Marcuse's "On the problem of the dialectic" ', *Telos* 27, 1976.
5. H. Marcuse, 'Contributions to a Phenomenology of Historical Materialism', *Telos* 4, 1969 (hereafter cited as 'Contributions'), p. 16.
6. *ibid*. p. 17.
7. Lipshires, *op. cit.* pp. 2-3, and Jay, *op. cit.* p.28.
8. H. Marcuse, 'The Foundation of Historical Materialism', *Studies in Critical Philosophy*, London: New Left Books 1972, p. 3.
9. *ibid*.

10. H. Marcuse, *Hegels Ontologie und die Grundlegung einer Theorie der Geschichtlichkeit*, Frankfurt am Main: V. Klostermann Verlag 1932.
11. *Studies in Critical Philosophy*, p. 12.
12. H. Marcuse, 'On the Philosophical Foundation of the Concept of Labor Economics', *Telos* 16, 1973 (hereafter cited as 'Economics'), pp. 30-31.
13. 'Economics', p. 17.
14. *ibid*. pp. 14-15.
15. On the origins of the Institute, P. Slater, *Origin and Significance of the Frankfurt School*, London: Routledge and Kegan Paul 1977; and Jay, *op. cit.*

2. Critical Rationality

1. 'Economics', p. 32 fn.
2. H. Marcuse, *Reason and Revolution*, London: Routledge and Kegan Paul 1969, p. 295.
3. *ibid*.
4. 'Contributions', p. 16.
5. H. Marcuse, *Negations*, Harmondsworth: Penguin 1972, p. 75.
6. 'Contributions', p. 18.
7. H. Marcuse, 'Das Problem der geschichtlichen Wirklichkeit', *Die Gesellschaft* VII, 4, 1931. See Jay, *op. cit.* p. 37.
8. *Reason and Revolution*, p. 37.
9. Quoted in Mehta, *op. cit.* p. 16.
10. K. Marx, *Capital I*, London: Lawrence and Wishart 1974, pp. 20-21.
11. K. Marx and F. Engels, *Collected Works* Vol. 3, London: Lawrence and Wishart 1975, p. 275; *Grundrisse*, Harmondsworth: Penguin 1973, pp. 161-62; *Capital I*, p. 458.
12. *Reason and Revolution*, p. 293.
13. K. Marx, *Capital III*, London: Lawrence and Wishart 1974, p. 820.
14. *Reason and Revolution*, pp. 316-17.
15. 'Economics', p. 31.
16. *Negations*, p. 132.
17. *Reason and Revolution*, pp. 43-46.
18. *Negations*, p. 136.
19. M. Horkheimer, 'On the Problem of Truth', in A. Arato and E. Gebhardt (eds.), *The Essential Frankfurt School Reader*, Oxford: Basil Blackwell 1978, p. 421.
20. *Negations*, p. 75.
21. *Reason and Revolution*, p. 126.
22. *ibid*. p. 313.
23. *ibid*. p. 281.
24. *ibid*. p. 282.
25. *Negations*, pp. 134-35.
26. *ibid*. p. 158.
27. H. Marcuse, 'Some Social Implications of Modern Technology', in Arato and Gebhardt, *op. cit.* (hereafter cited as 'Implications').

28. *Negations*, p. 152.
29. *Reason and Revolution*, p. 27.
30. *ibid*. p. 343.
31. *Negations*, p. 9.
32. *ibid*. p. 19.
33. *ibid*. p. 39.
34. *Collected Works* Vol. 3, p. 181.
35. *Negations*, p. 142.
36. K. Marx, *Early Writings*, Harmondsworth: Penguin 1975, p. 209.
37. *ibid*.
38. *Negations*, p. 154.
39. *ibid*.
40. *ibid*. pp. 117-18.
41. F. Schiller, *On the Aesthetic Education of Man*, Oxford: Clarendon Press 1967, p. 55.
42. *Negations*, pp. 120-21.
43. M. Horkheimer, *Critical Theory*, New York: The Seabury Press 1972, p. 289.
44. *Negations*, p. 95.
45. *ibid*. p. 98.
46. *ibid*. p. 132.
47. *ibid*. p. 131.
48. *Reason and Revolution*, p. 314.
49. *ibid*. p. 318.
50. *ibid*.
51. *ibid*. p. 317.
52. *Capital I*, p. 715.
53. *Negations*, p. 42.
54. *ibid*. p. 192.
55. *Studies in Critical Philosophy*, p. 136.
56. *ibid*.
57. *ibid*. p. 149.
58. *Critical Theory*, p. 215.
59. *Reason and Revolution*, p. 296.
60. Interview in B. Magee, *Men of Ideas*, London: BBC 1978, p. 68.
61. *ibid*.
62. *Negations*, p. 142.
63. *Critical Theory*, p. 234.
64. *Collected Works* Vol. 3, pp. 296-97.
65. *Reason and Revolution*, p. 293.
66. *ibid*. p. 322.

3. Eros.

1. T. W. Adorno in D. Fleming and B. Bailyn (eds.) *The Intellectual Migration*, Cambridge (Mass): Harvard 1969, p. 338.

2. B. Brecht, *Poems* Part 3, London: Eyre Methuen 1976, p. 367.
3. 'Implications', p. 143.
4. *ibid*. p. 155.
5. D. Kettler, 'The Vocation of Radical Intellectuals', *Politics and Society* Nov. 1970, p. 32.
6. *ibid*.
7. Lipshires, *op. cit*. p. 27.
8. Slater, *op. cit*. p. 95.
9. E. Fromm 'Method and Function of Analytical Social Psychology', in Arato and Gebhardt, *op. cit*. p. 478.
10. Slater, *op. cit*. p. 115.
11. *Negations*, p. 115.
12. *ibid*. p. 162.
13. *ibid*. p. 187.
14. *Studies in Critical Philosophy*, p. 179 (quoted from Sartre's *Being and Nothingness*).
15. *ibid*. pp. 179-80.
16. *Negations*, p. 116.
17. *Reason and Revolution*, p. 433.
18. H. Marcuse, *Eros and Civilization*, London: Abacus 1972, p. 75.
19. H. Marcuse, *Five Lectures*, London: Allen Lane 1970, p. 38.
20. *Eros and Civilization*, p. 39.
21. *ibid*. p. 47.
22. *ibid*. p. 42.
23. *ibid*. p. 75.
24. *ibid*. p. 49.
25. *ibid*. p. 24.
26. Arato and Gebhardt, *op. cit*. p. 523.
27. *Negations*, p. XV.
28. T. W. Adorno, *Prisms*, London: Neville Spearman 1967, p. 34.
29. *Eros and Civilisation*, p. 52.
30. *ibid*. p. 60.
31. *ibid*. p. 56.
32. *ibid*. p. 32.
33. K. Marx and F. Engels, *Selected Correspondence*, Moscow: Progress 1975, p. 435.
34. L. Trotsky, *The Revolution Betrayed*, New York: Pathfinder 1972, p. 112.
35. Lipshires, *op. cit*. p. 32.
36. *Eros and Civilization*, p. 147.
37. *ibid*. p. 145.
38. *Five Lectures*, p. 19.
39. *Eros and Civilization*, p. 50.
40. *ibid*. p. 44.
41. *ibid*. p. 124.
42. *ibid*. p. 125.
43. K. Marx and F. Engels, *Selected Works*, London: Lawrence and Wishart

1970, p. 494.
44. J. Lauritsen and D. Thorstad, *The Early Homosexual Rights Movement*, New York: Times Change 1974, p. 52.
45. *Bernstein on Homosexuality*, Belfast: Athol 1977; J. Weeks, *Coming Out*, London: Quartet 1977, pp. 145-47.
46. Weeks, *op. cit.* pp. 71-72.
47. Lauritsen and Thorstad, *op. cit.* p. 86.
48. *Eros and Civilization*, p. 145.
49. *ibid.* p. 146, 148.
50. *ibid.* p. 83.
51. *Grundrisse*, pp. 704-05.
52. *Eros and Civilization*, p. 136.
53. *ibid.* pp. 153-54.
54. *ibid.* p. 116.
55. Jay, *op. cit.* pp. 125-27; M. Poster, *Critical Theory of the Family*, London: Pluto 1978, pp. 53-58.
56. *Eros and Civilization*, p. 83.
57. *ibid.* p. 83.
58. *Grundrisse*, p. 705.
59. H. Marcuse, 'Preface' to R. Dunayevskaya, *Marxism and Freedom*, New York: Bookman Associates 1958, p. 15.
60. *ibid.* p. 20.
61. *Eros and Civilization*, p. 79.
62. *ibid.* p. 80.
63. *ibid.* p. 113.

4. Technological Rationality

1. 'Implications', pp. 156-57.
2. *ibid.* p. 141.
3. *ibid.* p. 143.
4. *ibid.* p. 145.
5. *ibid.* p. 149.
6. *ibid.* p. 150.
7. *ibid.* p. 151.
8. *ibid.* p. 154.
9. *ibid.*
10. *ibid.* p. 148.
11. *ibid.* p. 152.
12. H. Marcuse, *Soviet Marxism*, Harmondsworth: Penguin 1971, p. 73.
13. *ibid.*
14. *ibid.* p. 98.
15. *ibid.* p. 34.
16. *ibid.* p. 36.

17. *ibid.* p. 152.
18. K. Marx and F. Engels, *Collected Works* Vol. 6, London: Lawrence and Wishart 1976, p. 166.
19. H. Marcuse, *One-Dimensional Man*, London: Abacus 1972, p. 127.
20. *ibid.* p. 14.
21. *Negations*, pp. 223-24.
22. M. Horkheimer and T. W. Adorno, *Dialectic of Enlightenment*, London: Allen Lane 1973, p. 9.
23. *One-Dimensional Man*, p. 14.
24. S. Freud, *Civilization and its Discontents*, London: The Hogarth Press 1975, p. 58.
25. *Eros and Civilization*, p. 73.
26. *ibid.*
27. M. Heidegger, *Basic Writings*, London: Routledge and Kegan Paul 1978, p. 296.
28. *One-Dimensional Man*, p. 126.
29. *ibid.* p. 16.
30. 'Implications', p. 158.
31. *ibid.* p. 159.
32. *Soviet Marxism*, p. 110.
33. *ibid.* p. 111.
34. *One-Dimensional Man*, p. 62.
35. H. Marcuse, 'Remarks on a Redefinition of Culture', *Daedalus* 94, 1, 1965, p. 196.
36. *One-Dimensional Man*, pp. 72-73.
37. *ibid.* pp. 58-59.
38. K. Marx and F. Engels, *On Literature and Art*, Moscow: Progress 1976, p. 389.
39. A. Kettle (ed.), *The Nineteenth-Century Novel*, London: Heinemann, p. 72.
40. A. Orga, note to R.C.A. cassette Kachaturian: Symphony No. 1 (1979).
41. K. Miller 'The Point is Still to Change it', *Monthly Review*, 19, 2, 1967, p. 54.
42. *One-Dimensional Man*, p. 71.
43. T. W. Adorno, *Minima Moralia*, London: New Left Books 1974, p. 50.
44. *Five Lectures*, p. 49.
45. *One-Dimensional Man*, p. 13.
46. *Soviet Marxism*, p. 25.
47. *Selected Correspondence*, p. 103.
48. *Soviet Marxism*, p. 28.
49. *ibid.* pp. 31-32.
50. *One-Dimensional Man*, p. 33.
51. *ibid.*
52. *ibid.* p. 36.
53. *ibid.* p. 39.
54. *ibid.* p. 21.
55. 'Remarks on a Redefinition of Culture', p. 198.

56. *One-Dimensional Man*, p. 197.
57. *ibid*. pp. 49-51.
58. *ibid*. p. 48.
59. *ibid*. p. 49.
60. *ibid*. pp. 199-200.
61. H. Marcuse, 'Socialism in the Developed Countries', *International Socialist Journal* April 1965, p. 143.
62. *One-Dimensional Man*, p. 200.

5. Liberation

1. *Five Lectures*, p. 80.
2. H. Marcuse, 'Repressive Tolerance', in R. P. Wolff, B. Moore Jr. and H. Marcuse, *A Critique of Pure Tolerance*, Boston: Beacon 1969, p. 81.
3. *ibid*. p. 82.
4. *ibid*. p. 85.
5. H. Marcuse, 'Reply to Marshall Berman', *Partisan Review* 32, 1, 1965, p. 160.
6. *Five Lectures*, p. 86.
7. *ibid*. p. 83.
8. *ibid*. pp. 87-88.
9. H. Marcuse, *An Essay on Liberation*, Harmondsworth: Penguin 1972, p. 43.
10. *ibid*. p. 42.
11. *ibid*.
12. *Five Lectures*, p. 75.
13. H. Marcuse, 'Liberation from the Affluent Society', in D. Cooper (ed.), *The Dialectics of Liberation*, Harmondsworth: Penguin 1971, p. 191.
14. *An Essay on Liberation*, p. 62.
15. *ibid*. p. 52.
16. *ibid*. pp. 62-63.
17. *ibid*. p. 53.
18. *ibid*. p. 87.
19. *Soviet Marxism*, p. 41.
20. *An Essay on Liberation*, p. 84.
21. *Five Lectures*, p. 95.
22. *ibid*. p. 63.
23. H. Marcuse, 'The Paris Rebellion', *Peace News*, June 28 1968, p. 7.
24. *ibid*. p. 6.
25. *ibid*.
26. 'Implications', pp. 155-56.
27. *Five Lectures*, p. 81.
28. *An Essay on Liberation*, p. 61.
29. *ibid*. p. 30.
30. H. Marcuse, 'On the New Left', in M. Teodori, *The New Left: A Documentary History*, New York: Bobbs-Merrill 1969, p. 469.

31. H. Marcuse, 'Interview with Marcel Rioux', *Forces*, 22, 1973, p. 270.
32. 'La Liberté et l'ordre social', Textes des Conférences et des entretiens organisés par les Rencontres Internationales de Genève 1969, p. 270. Extract translated by Y. J. Le Juen.
33. H. Marcuse, *Counterrevolution and Revolt*, London: Allen Lane 1972, p. 25.
34. H. Marcuse, 'The Movement in a New Era of Repression', *Berkeley Journal of Sociology* XVI, 1971-72, p. 11.
35. *Counterrevolution and Revolt*, p. 9.
36. Quoted *ibid*. pp. 12-13; Marcuse also cited *Capital I*, pp. 476-77, and *Theories of Surplus Value* part I, London: Lawrence and Wishart 1969, pp. 156-57.
37. *Counterrevolution and Revolt*, p. 16.
38. *Grundrisse*, p. 325.
39. *Counterrevolution and Revolt*, p. 17.
40. *ibid*. p. 22.
41. *Eros and Civilization*, p. 153.
42. *One-Dimensional Man*, p. 184.
43. *Counterrevolution and Revolt*, p. 67.
44. *ibid*. pp. 68-69.
45. *ibid*. p. 69.
46. *ibid*.
47. H. Marcuse, *The Aesthetic Dimension*, Boston: Beacon 1978, pp. 71-72.
48. *Counterrevolution and Revolt*, p. 121.
49. *ibid*.

Conclusion

1. *Five Lectures*, p. 96.
2. *Negations*, pp. 80-81.

Select Bibliography

Zfs = *Zeitschrift für Sozialforschung*

Works by Marcuse

Schiller-Bibliographie unter Benutzung der Trämelschen Schiller-Bibliothek.
Berlin, S. Martin Fraenkel 1925.

'*Beiträge zur einer Phänomenologie des historischen Materialismus*',
Philosophische Hefte no. 1 1928, pp. 45-68. Translated as 'Contributions to a phenomenology of historical materialism', *Telos* 46, 1969,
pp. 3-34.

'*Zum Problem der Dialektik I*', *Die Gesellschaft*, Vol. VII 1930, part I, pp.
15-30.

'*Zum Problem der Dialektik II*', *Die Gesellschaft*, Vol. VIII 1931, part II,
pp. 541-57. III and IV translated as 'On the problem of the dialectic',
Telos 27, 1976.

Hegels Ontologie und die Grundlegung einer Theorie der Geschichtlichkeit,
Frankfurt am Main, V. Klostermann Verlag 1932.

'*Neue Quellen zur Grundlegung des Historischen Materialismus*' *Die
Gesellschaft* Vol IX, 8, August 1932. Translated as: 'The foundation of
historical materialism', in *Studies in Critical Philosophy*, London, New
Left Books 1972.

'*Uber die philosophischen Grundlagen des wirtschaftswissenschaftlichen
Arbeitsbegriffs*', *Archiv für Sozialwissenschaft und Sozialpolitik*, Vol.
69, 1933, pp. 257-92. Translated as: 'On the philosophical foundation
of the concept of labor in economics', *Telos* 16, 1973.

'*Der Kampf gegen den Liberalismus in der totalitären Staatsauffassung*', Zfs
III.1, 1934. Translated as 'The struggle against liberalism in the
totalitarian view of the state', in *Negations: Essays in Critical Theory*,
Harmondsworth, Penguin 1972.

'*Studien über Autorität und Familie*', *Studien über Autoritat und Familie*,
Paris, Libraire Félix Alcan, 1936. Translated as 'A study on authority',
in *Studies in Critical Philosophy*, op. cit. Written by various members
of the Institute of Social Research.

'*Zum Begriff des Wesens*', Zfs V.1, 1936. Translated as: 'The concept of
essence', in *Negations, op. cit.*

'*Uber den affirmativen Charakter der Kultur*', Zfs VI.1, 1937. Translated
as: 'The affirmative character of culture', in *Negations, op. cit.*

'*Philosophie und kritische Theorie*', Zfs VI.3, 1937. Translated as:
'Philosophy and critical theory', in *Negations, op. cit.*

'*Zur Kritik des Hedonismus*', Zfs VII.1, 1938. Translated as: 'On Hedonism', in *Negations, op. cit.*

'An introduction to Hegel's Philosophy', *Studies in Philosophy and Social Science* Vol. VIII 1940, pp. 394-412. Reprinted in *The Essential Frankfurt School Reader* edited by Arato, A. and Gebhardt, E., Oxford, Blackwell 1978.

Reason and Revolution, Oxford University Press 1941, 2nd ed. London, Routledge and Kegan Paul 1969.

'Some social implications of modern technology', *Studies in Philosophy and Social Science* Vol. IX, 1941, pp. 414-39.

'A rejoiner to K. Löwith's review of *Reason and Revolution*', *Journal of Philosophy and Phenomenological Research* Vol. II, No. 4, 1942, pp. 564-65.

'Existentialism: Remarks on Jean-Paul Sartre's l'Etre et le Néant', *Philosophy and Phenomenological Research* Vol VIII, No. 3 1949, reprinted as: 'Sartre's existentialism', *Studies in Critical Philosophy, op. cit.*

Review of *Essays on Freedom and Power* by Lord Acton, *American Historical Review*, 1949.

Review of *War and Human Progress: An Essay in the Rise of Industrial Civilisation* by John U. Nef, *American Historical Review*, 1951.

'Recent literature on communism', *World Politics* Vol. VI No. 4, 1954, pp. 515-25.

Supplementary chapter to *Reason and Revolution, op. cit.*

'Dialectics and logic since the war' in *Continuity and Change in Russian and Soviet Thought*, edited by Simmons, E.J., Cambridge, Mass., Harvard University Press 1955, pp. 347-58.

Eros and Civilisation, Boston, Beacon Press 1955, and London, Abacus 1972.

'Eros and culture', *The Cambridge Review* Vol. I No. 3, 1955, pp. 107-23.

'A reply to Erich Fromm', *Dissent* Vol. III No. 1 1956, pp. 79-81.

'*Trieblehre und Freiheit*', *Frankfurter Beitrage zur Soziologie*, Vol. 6, 1957; a lecture given in 1956 and translated as 'Freedom and Freud's Theory of Instincts' in *Five Lectures*, London, Allen Lane 1970.

Die Idee des Forschritts in Lichte der Psychoanalyse. Translated as 'Progress and Freud's theory of instincts' in *Five Lectures, op. cit.*

'The indictment of Western philosophy in Freud's theory', *Journal of Philosophy* 1957, pp. 154-55.

'Theory and therapy in Freud', *The Nation* Vol. 185, 28 September 1957, pp. 200-202.

Preface to F. Neumann *The Democratic and the Authoritarian State: Essays in Political and Legal Theory*, New York, Free Press 1964.

Preface to R. Dunayevskaya *Marxism and Freedom*, London, Pluto Press 1971.

Soviet Marxism, Columbia University Press 1958, and Harmondsworth, Pelican 1958.

'The ideology of death', in H. Feifel, *The Meaning of Death*, New York, McGraw Hill 1959.

'Notes on the problems of historical laws', *Partisan Review* Vol. 36 No. 1, 1959; reprinted as 'Karl Popper and the problem of historical laws', in *Studies in Critical Philosophy, op. cit.*

114

'Language and technological society', *Dissent* Vol. VIII No. 1 1961, pp. 66-74.

'The problem of social change in technological society', lecture presented to a UNESCO Symposium on Social Development. Limited distribution under auspices of Aron, R.P. and Hoselitz, B., Paris, 28 April 1961, pp. 139-60.

Review of George Lichtheim's *Marxism, an Historical and Critical Study*, *Political Science Quarterly* 77.1, 1962, pp. 117-19.

'The obsolescence of psychoanalysis', unpublished lecture of 1963; subsequently published as 'The obsolescence of the Freudian concept of man' in *Five Lectures, op. cit.*

'Thoughts on the defense of Gracchus Babeuf' in *The Defense of Gracchus Babeuf*, ed. Scott, J.A., Amherst, University of Massachusetts Press 1967.

'On science and phenomenology' in *Boston Studies in Philosophy and Science* II, 1964, pp. 279-80.

'World without logos', *Bulletin of the Atomic Scientists*, 20, 1964, pp. 25-26.

One-Dimensional Man, Boston, Beacon Press 1964, and London, Abacus 1972.

'Socialism in the developed countries' lecture given 1964, *International Socialist Journal*, Rome, April 1965.

'Industrialisation and capitalism in the work of Max Weber', trans. from German (1965), in *Negations op. cit.*

'Reply to Marshall Berman', *Partisan Review* 32 No. 1, 1965, pp. 159-61.

'Remarks on a redefinition of culture', *Daedalus* 94 No. 1 1965, pp. 190-207.

'On Vietnam', *Partisan Review* 32 No. 4, 1965, pp. 646-49.

'A tribute to Paul A. Baran', *Monthly Review*, No. II 1965, pp. 114-115.

'Socialist Humanism?', in E. Fromm *Socialist Humanism*, London, Allen Lane 1965.

Kultur und Gesellschaft Vols. 1 and 2, Frankfurt, Suhrkamp Verlag 1965.

'Repressive tolerance', in *A Critique of Pure Tolerance*, Wolff, R.P., Moore Jnr. B. and Marcuse, H., Boston, Beacon Press 1965.

'*The individual in the "Great Society"* ', *Alternatives* 1, 1966, pp. 14-146 and p. 20.

Political preface to *Eros and Civilisation* 1966, London, Abacus 1972.

'The concept of negation in the dialectic', written 1966, *Telos* 8, 1971, pp. 130-32.

'Ethics and revolution', in *Ethics and Society*, ed. de George, R.T., written 1966, London, Macmillan 1968.

'The obsolescence of marxism', in *Marx and the Western World*, ed. Lobkowitz, N., Notre Dame, Indiana, University of Notre Dame Press 1967.

'Art in one-dimensional society', *Arts Magazine* March 1967 reprinted in *Radical Perspectives in the Arts*, ed. Baxandall, L., Harmondsworth, Pelican 1972.

'Love mystified: A critique of Norman O. Brown', *Commentary* 1967, *Negations, op. cit.*

'*Das Ende der utopie*' lecture given July 1967. First published in

Psychoanalyse und Politik, Frankfurt 1968, trans. 'The end of Utopia', in *Five Lectures op. cit.*

'Das Problem der Gewalt in der Opposition' in *Psychoanalyse und Politik*, Frankfurt 1968. Translated as 'The problem of violence and the radical opposition', in *Five Lectures op. cit.*

'Liberation from the affluent society', lecture given July 1967, in *The Dialectics of Liberation*, ed. Cooper, D., Harmondsworth, Pelican 1968.

'On changing the world: a reply to Karl Miller', *Monthly Review*, 19 1967, pp. 42-48.

'The question of revolution', *New Left Review*, September-October 1967, pp. 3-7.

'Aggressiveness in advanced industrial society', translated from the German, 1968, in *Negations, op. cit.*

Interview with Marcuse, *New York Times*, 27 October 1968.

Negations: Essays in Critical Theory, London, Allen Lane 1968, and Harmondsworth, Penguin 1972.

'Postscript 1968', in *A Critique of Pure Tolerance*, Wolff, R.P., Moore Jnr, B. and Marcuse, H., 2nd ed. Boston, Beacon Press 1969.

An Essay on Liberation, Harmondsworth, Pelican 1972. Mostly written pre-May 1968.

'Re-examination of the concept of revolution', written 1968, *New Left Review*, July-August 1969, pp. 27-34.

'The Paris rebellion', *Peace News* 28 June 1968, pp. 6-7.

Interview with R. McKenzie, *The Listener*, 17 October 1968.

'On the New Left', speech given December 1968, in *The New Left: A Documentary History*, ed. Teodori, M., New York, Bobbs-Merrill 1969.

'Freedom and the historical imperative', written 1969, in *Studies in Critical Philosophy, op. cit.*

'The realm of freedom and the realm of necessity — a reconsideration', *Praxis* 5, Nos. 1 & 2, 1969, pp. 20-25.

'Revolutionary subject and self-government', *Praxis* 5, Nos. 1 and 2, 1969, pp. 326-29.

'Marxism and the new humanity: an unfinished revolution', lecture given April 1969, in *Marxism and Radical Religion: Essays Toward a Revolutionary Humanism*, ed. Raines, J.C. and Dean, T., Philadelphia, Temple University Press 1970.

'*La Liberté et l'ordre social*'. Textes des Conférences et es entretiens organises par les Rencontres Internationales de Genève, 1969, pp. 121-43.

'Art as a form of reality', talk given 1969, *New Left Review*, July-August 1972, pp. 51-88.

'Revolution out of disgust', translated from German in *Der Spiegel*, 28 July 1969, *Australian Left Review*, December 1969, pp. 36-47.

'Essay on art', in *On the Future of Art*, ed. Fry, E. New York, Viking Press 1970.

'Charles Reich — a negative view', *New York Times*, 6 November 1970, p.41.

Five Lectures, London, Allen Lane 1970.

116

Open Letter, in A. Davis *If They Come in the Morning*, London, Orbach and Chambers 1971.

'The Movement in a New Era of Repression, lecture 1971, *Berkeley Journal of Sociology* XVI, 1971-72, pp. 1-14.

'A conversation with Herbert Marcuse'. Interview with Kean, S. and Raser, J. *Psychology Today*, February 1971, pp. 35-39 and p.60.

'Reflections on Calley', *New York Times*, 13 May 1971, p.45.

'A reply to Lucien Goldmann', *Partisan Review* 38 Winter 1971-72, pp. 397-400.

Studies in Critical Philosophy, London, New Left Books 1972.

Counter Revolution and Revolt, London, Allen Lane 1972.

Die Permanenz der Kunst: Wider eine bestimmte Marxistische Aesthetik, Munich, Carl Hanser Verlag 1977. Translated as *The Aesthetic Dimension: Toward a Critique of Marxist Aesthetics*, Boston, Beacon Press 1978.

Interview with Bryan Magee 'Marcuse and the Frankfurt School' in *Men in Ideas* edited by Magee, B, London, BBC 1978.

Works on Marcuse in English

Andrew, E. 'Work and freedom in Marcuse and Marx', *Canadian Journal of Political Science*, Vol III June 1970.

Andrew, E. 'A reply to William Leiss, Technological Rationality: Notes on "Work and Freedom in Marcuse and Marx" ', *Canadian Journal of Political Science*, Vol. IV, September 1971.

Arato. A and Gebhardt. E (eds) *The Essential Frankfurt School Reader* Oxford Blackwell 1978.

Batalov, E. *The Philosophy of Revolt*, Moscow, Progress 1975.

Berki, R.N. 'Notes on Marcuse and the idea of tolerance', in *Dissent and Disorder: Essays in Social Theory*, ed. Parekh, B., Toronto, W.U.S. of Canada 1971.

Berki, R.N. 'Marcuse and the crisis of the new radicalism: from politics to religion?', *The Journal of Politics* 34, 1972.

Berman, M. Review of *One-Dimensional Man*, *Partisan Review* IV, 1964. 'Reply to Marcuse' *Partisan Review* I, 1965.

Bernstein, R.J. 'Herbert Marcuse: an immanent critique', *Social Theory and Practice* I, Fall 1971.

Bethune, D.McL. 'The politics of liberation: the political philosophy of Herbert Marcuse', Ph.D. thesis, Tulane University 1974.

Breines, P. *Critical Interruptions. New Left Perspectives on Herbert Marcuse*, New York, Herder and Herder 1972.

Bronner, S.E. 'Art and utopia: the Marcusian perspective', *Politics and Society* 3, Winter 1973.

Bykhovskii, B. 'Marcusism against marxism - a critique of uncritical criticism', *Philosophy and Phenomenological Research* XXX no. 2, 1969.

Campbell, K. 'Marcuse on the justification of revolution', *Politics* (Australasia) November 1969.

Castro, F. Report of speech attacking Marcuse (amongst others), *New York Times* 26 July 1970.

Clayre, A. 'Marcuse and revolution', *The Observer* 18 May 1969.

Cohen, J. 'Critical theory: the philosophy of Marcuse', *New Left Review* 57, September-October 1969.

Colletti, L. 'From Hegel to Marcuse', in *From Rousseau to Lenin*, London New Left Books 1972.

Connerton, P. 'Shooting at the clocks', *The Listener* 83 5 February 1970.

Connerton, P. *Critical Sociology*, Harmondsworth, Penguin 1976

Connerton, P. *The Tragedy of Enlightenment*, Cambridge, Cambridge University Press 1980.

Cranston, M. 'Herbert Marcuse', in *The New Left*, London, The Bodley Head 1970.

Dahl, L.H. 'Marcuse on the individual in the advanced industrial society,' Ph.D. thesis, Southern Illinois University 1974.

Davis, A. *An Autobiography*, London, Arrow Books 1976.

Delaney, P. 'Marcuse in the Seventies', *Partisan Review* III, 1973.

Deutscher, I. *On Socialist Man*, New York, Merit 1967.

Duclow, D. 'Herbert Marcuse and "happy consciousness" ', *Liberation* XIV, 1969.

Dutschke, R. Statement of solidarity with Marcuse, *Australian Left Review*, December 1969.

Eidelberg, P. 'The temptation of Herbert Marcuse', *Review of Politics* 31, no. 4, 1969.

Fischer, G. (ed) *The Revival of American Socialism*, New York, Oxford University Press, 1971.

Fry, J. *Marcuse: Dilemma and Liberation*, Brighton, Harvester Press 1978.

Gibson, H.C. *Marcuse: From Logos to Eros*, Ph.D. thesis, University of Hull 1976.

Glaser, K. 'Marcuse and the German New Left', *National Review* 2 July 1968.

Goldmann, L. 'Understanding Marcuse', *Partisan Review* III, 1971.

Graubard, J.A. 'One-Dimensional Pessimism', *Dissent* XV 3 1968.

Graubard, J.A. *The Political Position of Herbert Marcuse*, Ph.D. thesis, Harvard University 1968.

Greeman, R. 'A critical re-examination of Herbert Marcuse's works', *New Politics* VI, Fall 1967.

Held, D. *Introduction to Critical Theory* London, Hutchinson 1980.

Horowitz, M. 'Portrait of the marxist as an old trooper', *Playboy*, September 1970.

Jameson, F. *Marxism and Form*, Oxford, Oxford University Press 1971.

Jay, M. 'The metapolitics of utopianism', *Dissent* XVII 4, 1970.

Jay, M. *The Dialectical Imagination*, London, Heinemann Educational Books 1974.

Kateb, G. 'The political thought of Herbert Marcuse', *Commentary* 49, January 1970.

Kellner, D. 'Introduction to "On the philosophical foundation of the concept of labor" ', *Telos* 16 1973.

Kettler, D. 'The vocation of radical intellectuals', *Politics and Society* November 1970.

Kettler, D. 'Herbert Marcuse: the critique of bourgeois civilization and its transcendence', in *Contemporary Political Philosophers*, de Crespigny, A. and Minogue, K., London, Methuen 1976.

King, R. *The Party of Eros: Radical Social Thought and the Realm of Freedom*, Chapel Hill (N.C.) University of North Carolina Press, 1972.

Lichtheim, G. 'From Marx to Hegel: reflections on Georg Lukács, T.W. Adorno and Herbert Marcuse', *Triquarterly*, July 1968.

Lichtheim, G. *Collected Essays*, New York, Viking Press 1973.

Lipshires, S.S. *Herbert Marcuse: From Marx to Freud and Beyond*, Cambridge Mass., Schenkmann Publishing Company 1974.

Lloyd, M.J. 'The negative philosopher', Month 2, October 1970.

McInnes, N. *The Western Marxists*, London, The Alcove Press 1972.

MacIntyre, A. *Marcuse*, London, Fontana 1970.

Marks, R.W. *The Meaning of Marcuse*, New York, Ballantyne 1972.

Mattick, P. *Critique of Marcuse*, London, Merlin 1972.

Miller, K. 'The point is still to change it', *Monthly Review* Vol 19 No. 2, 1967.

Parekh, B. 'Utopianism and Manicheanism: a critique of Marcuse's theory of revolution', *Social Research* 39 Winter 1972.

Piccone, P. and Delfini, A. 'Marcuse's Heideggerian Marxism', *Telos* 6 1970.

Robinson, P. *The Sexual Radicals*, St. Albans, Granada Books 1972.

Schneider, C.D. 'Utopia and history: Herbert Marcuse and the logic of revolution', *Philosophy Today* 12, 1968.

Schoolman, M. 'Introduction to Marcuse's *On the problem of the dialectic*', *Telos* 27 1976.

Sedgwick, P. 'Natural science and human theory', in *Socialist Register* 1966.

Shapiro, J.J. 'From Marcuse to Habermas', *Continuum* VIII, Spring-Summer 1970.

Slater, P. *The Origin and Significance of the Frankfurt School*, London, Routledge and Kegan Paul, 1977.

Sparrow, J. 'Marcuse and the gospel of hate', *Spectator*, 9 August 1969.

Therborn, G. 'The Frankfurt School', *New Left Review*, October 1970.

Vivas, E. *Contra Marcuse*, New Rochelle (N.Y.), Arlington House 1971.

Walsh, J.L. 'Why Marcuse matters', *Commonweal*, XCIII 2 October 1970.

Walton, P. 'From surplus value to surplus theories: Marx, Marcuse and MacIntyre', *Social Research* Vol 37 (4) 1970.

Walton, P. and Gamble, A. 'Herbert Marcuse' in *From Alienation to Surplus Value*, London, Sheed and Ward 1973.

Wiatr, J.J. 'Herbert Marcuse: philosopher of a lost radicalism', *Science and Society* XXXIV, Fall 1970.

Wilden, A. 'Marcuse and the Freudian Model: Energy, Information and Phantasie', The Legacy of the German Refugee Intellectuals, *Salmagundi* 10/11 Fall 1969 -Winter 1970.

Woddis, J. *New Theories of Revolution*, London, Lawrence and Wishart 1972.

Wolff, K.H. and Moore Jnr. B. (eds.) *The Critical Spirit: Essays in Honor of Herbert Marcuse*, Boston, Beacon Press 1967.

Zamoshkin, A. and Motroshilova, N.V. 'Is Marcuse's critical theory of society critical?', *Soviet Review* 11, Spring 1970.

Zhukov, Y. 'Taking Marcuse to the woodshed' *Atlas* 16, 1968.

Index